# NINE MEN AGAINST AMERICA

# NINE MEN
# AGAINST AMERICA

*The Supreme Court
and Its Attack on American Liberties*

R O S A L I E   M.   G O R D O N

THE DEVIN-ADAIR COMPANY • NEW YORK
1958

CANADIAN AGENT: THOMAS NELSON & SONS, LTD., TORONTO
LIBRARY OF CONGRESS CATALOGUE CARD NUMBER: 58–9754
MANUFACTURED IN THE UNITED STATES OF AMERICA

TO JOHN T. FLYNN

*Who is in no way responsible for this book, but without whose shining example, over many long years, of the true traditions of American journalism, it could not have been written.*

# CONTENTS

# FOREWORD

"It has long been my opinion, and I have never shrunk from its expression . . . that the germ of dissolution of our federal government is in the constitution of the federal judiciary; an irresponsible body—for impeachment is scarcely a scarecrow—working like gravity by night and by day, gaining a little today and a little tomorrow, and advancing its noiseless step like a thief, over the field of jurisdiction, until all shall be usurped from the States, and the government of all be consolidated into one.

"To this I am opposed; because, when all government, domestic and foreign, in little as in great things, shall be drawn to Washington as the center of all power, it will render powerless the checks provided of one government or another, and will become as venal and oppressive as the government from which we separated."

THOMAS JEFFERSON, 1821.

*NINE MEN AGAINST AMERICA*

# CHAPTER ONE

# What the Attack Means to American Liberties

You are an American. You love your country. You think it is the greatest and finest nation on earth. You feel, of course, that there is plenty wrong with it but that, after all is said, somehow we will always come out on top. You seldom think consciously about it, but you feel you have the protection of such a charter of freedom as man has never before known. It guarantees to you a system of government and a mode of life which, whatever their faults, have brought you the highest degree of freedom and abundance among all the world's inhabitants.

Then, one day, quite by accident, you are shocked out of your complacence. You pay a visit to your son's schoolroom. His teacher is expounding to the class—including your son—some theories that sound strangely alien to you. They *are* alien to sound American thinking, but this teacher doesn't label them as such. He seems to be telling your son and his fellow students that these theories are the right ones—the best ones. Sorely troubled, you go to the principal. You say:

"Who is this man? He sounds like a communist to me —or at least a fellow traveler."

The principal answers: "He is."

You look astonished: "Then what's he doing here—in a public school that I help support with my taxes?"

"We fired him," the principal says. "We have a law in this state that a teacher in one of our schools who is called before an investigating committee and hides behind the Fifth Amendment to conceal his communist connections is subject to immediate dismissal."

"Then how did he get back in here?" you want to know.

"The Supreme Court of the United States made us reinstate him in his job—with back pay, too!"

Or you overhear one day a conversation among three or four men. It might go something like this:

First Man: "We couldn't trust too many. We'd have to use them carefully."

Second Man: "We don't need many—just our hard core who have been thoroughly trained. We place them in strategic spots."

Third Man: "They're all well indoctrinated with revolutionary techniques. We've done a pretty good job on the softening-up process—and now we can even talk openly about overthrowing the government, if that should be necessary."

Second Man: "And our group can handle both—the propaganda, and the action when the time comes."

First Man: "What are the strategic spots?"

Third Man: "We won't discuss that too exactly. But generally let's say New York, Chicago, L.A., and, of course, Washington, D.C., and maybe a few others."

You wait to hear no more. You rush to the nearest office of the FBI. You tell the agent in charge what you have heard. You describe the men as well as you can. The agent looks at you sadly. He says: "Yes, we know the men. We've been watching them for a long time."

"Then why don't you arrest them?" you demand.

"A while back we could," he replies. "Congress gave us a law under which native enemies of America who advocated the overthrow of the government could be indicted and prosecuted. But now—now it's different. The Supreme Court says that when these saboteurs talk about overthrowing the government, they can't be touched. We have to wait until they spell out specifically how they're going to do it and actually try it. And then—."

"And then," you finish, "it might be too late."

Or perhaps you need an attorney to handle a small matter for you. You pick one at random from the accredited list in your state and go to see him. You aren't talking to him long before you realize that if you give this man your case, you will have a communist representing you. You leave his office in a rage and go to your State Bar Association. You demand to know how this young man, only just out of law school, can be an accredited attorney in your state—particularly in the face of all we now know about the communist conspiracy. The Bar Association official patiently explains to you that the Bar Examining Board in your state has had a rule for some time that any would-be lawyer who is a known communist or who refuses to say whether he has communist connections is *not* admitted to the bar and permitted to practice before your courts. BUT—he says, that *was* the rule. Now the Supreme Court of the United States has stepped in and told us—a sovereign American state— that we cannot set the standards for who shall and shall not practice law before our own courts. In other words, the Court says we can't keep a man from taking the bar examination in this state because he is a communist.

By this time your mind is in a whirl. What's going on, you ask yourself. What's happening to us—to me, to my country? Surely something is wrong somewhere. You've never had too much use for politicians generally—you consider them a more or less necessary evil. But one thing you know—when all else fails, there has always been one last resort for the protection of Americans. It is in the Congress of the United States—your elected representatives—and particularly in the congressional power of investigation—the power of exposure of wrongdoing and subversion and other evils.

So you go to see your congressman. You start to tell him of your experiences. Then you notice an odd expression on his face. You stop. Despairingly you ask—"You don't mean—you can't mean—?"

"The Supreme Court?" he answers. "Yes, we on the congressional investigating committees have been getting it too. You know, throughout our history, Congress has always had the right to question witnesses. If they wanted to, they could protect themselves with the Fifth Amendment against self-incrimination. But when any subversive or grafter refused to answer other questions, we could cite him for contempt. And our courts have generally backed us up. We were the last resort for Americans to get the information they must have to protect their lives, their liberty, and their property."

"But now—" he sighed, "now the Supreme Court says that before we can make a witness answer questions, we have to spell out for him not only the exact purpose of our committee but also the exact pertinence of the question to that purpose. Just imagine! We investigate in order to get for ourselves and our constituents—you—the information we need to write necessary legislation. But now, according to the Supreme Court, we have to know exactly what we're going to do and how we're going to do it—and explain it all explicitly to the witness—before we get out of him the information we need in order to decide what we're going to do and how to do it! You can see that the Supreme Court has just about put an end to our investigative powers. Certainly it has crippled them almost fatally."

All this and very much more—actual assaults on the liberties of Americans and on their means of protecting themselves against tyranny from within and without—has been brought about by a Supreme Court composed of nine men—nine men against 170 million Americans. Who are these men? What makes them tick? How did it come about that so few—these particular few—were in the right spot at the right time to do so much harm? What is it they have done? And how have they done it? How does it affect you, your children, your business, your job, and your freedom? We must know the answers to these questions, because the future of our country—the country we love—is at stake.

# CHAPTER TWO

# The Seeds of the Attack Are Sown

The story begins a long time ago, but within the clear memory of many living Americans—in the year 1937. Franklin D. Roosevelt was President of the United States. He had just been reelected for a second term. During his first term, in a complete reversal of all his campaign promises, he demanded of Congress a set of laws which would change the entire concept and nature of our form of government and our way of doing business.

In the intervening decades since Roosevelt's first election—years of depression, communist infiltration, socialist revolution, and war—it has been forgotten that Roosevelt was elected in 1932 on what was essentially a conservative platform. It is one of the ironies of history that the man who denounced Herbert Hoover as a "spendthrift," who made ringing demands for economy in government, who as governor of New York made impassioned pleas for the rights of the sovereign states, would become the architect and first leader of America's slide into a European-type authoritarian system of government.

The American Republic had been established as a shining beacon to freedom-loving peoples all over the world. Not the least of its attractions, of course, was the fact that it also brought to free men the greatest abundance ever known. Since it *was* a free system—and was made up of free human beings—it had its periods of recession and depression, but not even in their most severe aspects did they ever sink to the level of congenital poverty of the European systems from which our people fled.

With all its faults, Americans were wedded—for better or for worse—to our American way of life. And in 1932, despite almost three years of severe economic depression, they elected Franklin D. Roosevelt to the presidency, believing they were naming a man who would bring about whatever adjustments and reforms were necessary *within the framework of the American system*. That is what the candidate had told them he would do. It is true that the people were demanding that something be done about the economic crisis; they believed—mistakenly—that Hoover was doing nothing, and they wanted a change. But they did not want a change from the American system to some collectivist system. If they had, they could have voted for Norman Thomas and his outspokenly socialist program—as some 800,000 of them did.

By the time Roosevelt took office, in March 1933, the economic disaster, with the closing of the banks, was complete. He made one feeble attempt to carry out a campaign promise by asking, and getting, from Congress a 25-percent reduction in government expenses. That took care of the platform on which he was elected. He then proceeded to act as though it had never existed, and we had the circus of "the hundred days," in which, helped along by the severity of the depression, Roosevelt prevailed upon a compliant Congress to pass a batch of laws completely alien to our form of government and our free-enterprise economic system. They were supposed to end the depression. In fact, they were sold to the people on that basis by the growing coterie of left-wing philosophers who surrounded the President. But they didn't end the depression. If anything, they prolonged it, because they were designed not to restore health to our traditional system but to confuse it, undermine it, and eventually to destroy it.

Our latter-day New Dealers and "liberals" are fond of declaring that, no matter what else may be said of Roosevelt, he did "end the depression." And, after the manner of Hitler's Big Lie, they have repeated this over and over again so often, even imbedding it in the majority of textbooks used in our schools, that today millions of people believe it. Yet, when World War II broke out in Europe —seven years after Roosevelt's first election—*there were as many unemployed people in America as on the day he took office.* It was by embroiling us with Europe and eventually dragging us into the war that Roosevelt "ended the depression"—not with his myriad New Deal schemes and laws.

# CHAPTER THREE

# The Court and Our Freedom

The New Deal laws were challenged in our courts and, in the course of time, they reached the Supreme Court of the United States. The Supreme Court, during our years as a nation, had commanded great respect among most Americans. Americans were aware, consciously or subconsciously, that it stood as the final bulwark against any attempts to tamper with the charter of our liberties—the Constitution. That is not to say, of course, that the Supreme Court always acted wisely or even constitutionally throughout our history. But in the last twenty years it has arrogated to itself new powers and taken us on a headlong plunge into authoritarian government. The descent has been swiftest in most recent years particularly, as we shall see.

The Supreme Court was set up by the founders of our Republic to settle disputes as to the meaning of the Constitution, and laws made under it which affected the rights of individual citizens and of the sovereign American states. In other words, the Supreme Court's job was to *interpret* our Constitution and laws *according to the very special type of government which that Constitution blueprints.*

Ours is a unique form of government. There never has been anything like it. The Constitution not only guaranteed to each American the greatest individual freedom ever known to man, but it gave to us a system of government that could make good on the guarantee.

Put simply, ours is a federal system. In the beginning there was no central government. There were thirteen sovereign states—thirteen independent republics. They banded together and created a federal government for their own protection against foreign enemies, for the protection of each state as against other states, and for the protection of each citizen within each state as against the citizens of other states. The federal government was the *creature of the states.* To make sure that it would never become powerful enough to oppress either the states or their citizens, it was given very limited powers. And those powers were broken up among three independent agencies—the Executive (the President), the Congress (the Senate representing the states and the House representing the individual citizens of the states), and the Judiciary (the federal courts).

This was the first and only system of government in history which made *impossible* the growth of an all-powerful central government. Only under an all-powerful central government—be it republic, monarchy, democracy, or dictatorship—can the forces of communist or socialist or fascist tyranny operate. *They must have complete central authority;* otherwise their tyranny cannot withstand the revolt of men who wish to be free.

The Supreme Court of the United States was created to see to it that if the Congress or the President or both should ever attempt to impose laws on the people or the sovereign states which did not conform to the Constitution, the Court would declare them invalid—unconstitutional—and therefore null and void.

And so, during President Roosevelt's first term, as one by one the laws which he had induced Congress to pass came before the Supreme Court, it applied to them that constitutional test—and declared nearly all of them unconstitutional.

# CHAPTER FOUR

# *"The Nine Old Men"*

The Court at the time was made up of a distinguished panel of jurists. They represented all shades of opinion—from the so-called conservatism of Justices Sutherland, Van Devanter, McReynolds, and Butler, to the so-called liberalism of Brandeis, Stone, and Cardozo. A middle philosophy was represented by Justice Roberts and Chief Justice Charles Evans Hughes.

Members of Supreme Courts have not always had an overabundance of previous judicial experience. But, generally speaking, most presidents who had an opportunity to make appointments to our highest court sensed that at least a few of the nine justices should have had either a wide judicial background or a thorough grounding in constitutional law, or both. The assumption used to be, when we were still consciously operating under constitutional government, that the Court had been conceived as a single, independent arm of government, rather than as a group of prima donnas, and that whatever judicial experience there was among the members would be at the service of all other members of the Court.

While the Supreme Court which decided the early New Deal cases was not overburdened with individual judicial experience, collectively it had a backlog to draw upon which our three "liberal" or "modern" presidents, Roosevelt, Truman, and Eisenhower, have since failed to match in any of their appointments. On the so-called conservative side, Justice Willis Van Devanter had been a United States circuit judge for eight years and had served as chief justice of the Supreme Court of Wyoming. On the so-called liberal side, Justice Benjamin Cardozo had been a judge of the Court of Appeals of New York and then its chief judge, and had served a long term on the New York Supreme Court (which is a lower court in New York State). In the case of the Chief Justice —in whom previous judicial experience would seem almost mandatory—Charles Evans Hughes had already served, years before, as an associate justice of the United States Supreme Court. He had also been a professor of law at Cornell University and Secretary of State in two cabinets.

There was, of course, in the Court which Chief Justice Hughes headed, a definite cleavage between the conservatives and the liberals. (The term "liberal" did not then have the left-wing content that it has today.) While the so-called liberal justices—Stone, Brandeis, and Cardozo—perhaps could not be called strictly liberals in the 19th-century meaning of the word—when a liberal meant simply a defender of the individual's liberty against government—they were by no means modern "liberals," despite their subsequent adoption as heroes by the minions of the left. The leftists have taken up Justice Brandeis, for instance, in a large way because of his opposition to bigness in business. They conveniently overlook the fact that he was equally opposed to bigness in government. Essentially, men of the type of Stone, Brandeis, and Cardozo were for reform—and God knows, reform was needed at the time—and for some degree of "social welfare" for the masses of the people. They were not alone in failing to foresee the strange bypaths down which we would be led when "social welfare" became a tool in the kit of vote-conscious politicians. But whether it was reform, or "social welfare" or so-called "civil rights," they and their colleagues on the bench thought of it all *within the framework of the American constitutional system.* As was only human, some of them could stretch their interpretations of the Constitution pretty far to suit their own proclivities, but they knew the Constitution was there, plus the long body of precedent in law established by previous Supreme Courts. They did not, as later Courts were to do, ever consider the Constitution a mere scrap of paper to be tossed out the window whenever they chose to arrogate to themselves those powers which were intended only for the Congress or the states or which remained in the people until such time as they chose to delegate them by constitutional amendment.

In other words, the Court composed of Hughes, Stone, Brandeis, Cardozo, Sutherland, Van Devanter, Butler, Roberts, and McReynolds was made up of men well versed in constitutional law. Whatever their opinions, their philosophy was basically American. Nowhere was this better illustrated than in their action on the most important of the early New Deal laws—the National Recovery Act (NRA).

In the NRA, Congress had handed over to the President dictatorial powers by which the central government would have complete control in the management and regulation of every phase of American industry—big and little—from the smallest tailor shop in an American town to the giant steel industry. Although most Americans did not realize it at the time, the NRA was patterned almost exactly after the fascist corporative state which Mussolini had set up in Italy.

The hearing on the constitutionality of the NRA before the Supreme Court, serious as it was, had its comic aspects. The matter came to the Court in the A.L.A. Schechter v. U.S. case, popularly known as the "Sick Chicken" case. Under the NRA, the federal government set up code authorities (in Fascist Italy they were called corporatives) which made rules and regulations for the governing of each phase of each and every industry. The purpose was to regulate hours, wages, working conditions, trade practices, prices, and everything else that could be thought up by the fertile mind of a government bureaucrat. In the code set up for the live-poultry business in and around metropolitan New York, one rule provided that diseased and uninspected poultry could not be sold. (This was the height of redundancy, since there already were stringent federal, state, and local laws on this very subject.) Another rule—set up to do away with the free market in poultry and to keep prices firm—decreed that buyers could not pick and choose among chickens in each coop. If they did, the first buyers would get the best fowl and the remaining fowl might have to be sold at a lower price. Price cutting was anathema to the NRA planners.

The NRA cracked down on a certain poultry dealer, A.L.A. Schechter, for violating its rules and convicted him—with a fine and a jail sentence—on two counts: selling diseased poultry and violating its rule against "straight killing." When the case reached the Supreme Court, the defendant explained that under "straight killing" a buyer had to put his hand in the coop and take whatever chicken he touched first—he couldn't pick and choose. Mr. Justice McReynolds, in amazement, asked the defendant's counsel: "And it was for that your client was convicted?"

"Yes, and fined and given a jail sentence," replied the lawyer. He went on to explain that if a customer wanted only half a coop of chickens, he had to take them just as they came to him—no choosing. Whereupon Justice Sutherland, from the bench, inquired: "What if the chickens are all at one end?" The answer was drowned out in a gale of laughter from the bar and the audience, in which all the justices joined.

The charge that the poultry dealer had sold diseased fowl was based on the sale of a hen which had passed federal inspection. She wasn't diseased; she was just, in the language of the trade, "eggbound."

This incident was matched by many others during those hectic days of the Blue Eagle—the badge of compliance with NRA directives. One man was arrested, indicted, put in jail for several days, and then required to

put up bond for violating a law that didn't exist. A little
tailor gained momentary fame when he was sent to jail
for pressing a pair of pants for 35 cents—five cents below
the code minimum of 40 cents.

But the NRA involved a great deal more than price-
cutting pants pressers and eggbound chickens. It was a
clumsy attempt to hand over to the federal bureaucrats
limitless powers over every phase of our economic life.

*All nine justices of the Supreme Court joined unani-
mously in declaring the NRA unconstitutional.* Chief
Justice Hughes, speaking for the entire Court, declared:
"We think that the code-making authority thus conferred [on the President] is an unconstitutional delegation of legislative power." And Justice Cardozo added:
"This is delegation running riot."

Then in rather rapid succession came decisions declaring unconstitutional other New Deal laws, such as the
AAA, which was designed to wrap the tentacles of federal control around agriculture and farming in the same
manner as the NRA had done around industry; and the
Bituminous Coal Act, an attempt to control, separately,
the workings of the coal industry.

The Bituminous Coal Act was a particularly flagrant
case of Roosevelt's defiance—or ignorance—of the Constitution. Congress had hesitated about passing the law
because of doubts as to its constitutionality. Roosevelt
thereupon wrote the chairman of the committee in charge
of the bill to go ahead and pass it anyway. He said: "I
hope your committee will not permit doubts as to constitutionality, no matter how reasonable, to block the suggested legislation."

Actually, many of the New Deal laws which the Court declared unconstitutional had been creating such a shambles in our economic and social life that it came as something of a relief, even to many members of the New Deal inner circle, when the Court killed them.

But President Roosevelt was angry. He began to vilify the Court and its members. He spoke sneeringly of them as a "horse-and-buggy court." This vilification—personified in the derisive phrase "the nine old men"—was taken up and expanded in the press, in magazines, and on the radio by the New Deal cohorts and the growing advocates in high places of the socialist revolution. These advocates saw with clarity that America could never be turned into a centrally dominated collectivist society so long as the Constitution stood as the supreme law of the land and the judges of the Supreme Court interpreted it according to its intended meaning.

Immediately following President Roosevelt's second inauguration, one of his first acts was to launch an all-out attack on the Supreme Court. He demanded of Congress a law by which he might be allowed to appoint a new judge to the Court for every judge then sitting who was 70 years of age or more and thus bring the membership of the Court from nine up to 15. This would have allowed Roosevelt at once to appoint six New Deal justices to nullify the votes on the Court of six sitting judges who were 70 years of age. In this way he could get his unconstitutional New Deal schemes declared valid.

This, of course, was the famous "court-packing" plan. It set off one of the greatest debates in the history of Congress. Mr. Roosevelt thought he had Congress in

the palm of his hand, but his plan was too much even for
that submissive New Deal body. The fight against the
court-packing proposal was actually led by members of
Mr. Roosevelt's own party and after months of angry debate it was killed.

President Roosevelt once tried to make a deal with
Chief Justice Hughes, by which Hughes would talk over
with him constitutional issues that were before the Court,
in return for which Roosevelt would clear proposed legislation with the Chief Justice. Any law clerk could have
pointed out to the President the impropriety of such a
proposal. But, to Roosevelt, the Chief Justice's coolness
to the idea was simply evidence of the Court's "unwilling-
ness to cooperate."

Roosevelt persisted in trying to put over the court-packing plan even after it became evident that Congress was
not going to do his bidding. In the process, he alienated
some of the so-called liberal justices who were inclined to
regard at least some of the New Deal laws with a kindly
eye. While the NRA decision had been unanimous, in
some subsequent cases Brandeis, Stone, and Cardozo dissented. And in the midst of the court-packing fight several other New Deal laws were validated by these three
with an assist from Chief Justice Hughes and Justice
Roberts. Some observers of the time remarked, perhaps
unfairly, that Supreme Court justices not only follow the
election returns; they read the newspapers and harbor an
interest in their "job status"—even as the least of us.

The New Dealers promptly dubbed the dissenters
in these later cases—Van Devanter, McReynolds, Sutherland, and Butler—"the Four Horsemen of Reaction."

The leftists gleefully pointed the finger of scorn at Justice Butler because he had become a millionaire, before his appointment to the Court, through his legal services for great railroads. They sneered at Justices Van Devanter and Sutherland because of their old-fashioned "frontier roots" in our western states. Justice Van Devanter, born in Indiana in 1859, had later migrated to Wyoming, where he became a member of the territorial legislature before Wyoming was admitted to the Union. After his adopted state achieved statehood, he became, in 1889, Chief Justice of Wyoming's Supreme Court. George Sutherland, born in England in 1862, had settled in Utah with his parents. He became a member, in 1896, of the first Utah Senate. But the leftists kept silent about the fortune Justice Brandeis had made in the practice of corporation law and the fact that Justice Stone was a New Hampshire farm boy who became a Wall Street lawyer, director of large corporations, and an intimate of the Morgan partners.

Actually, the court of that day represented a fair cross-section of America. But the leftists were bent on dividing us into the "downtrodden masses" and the "economic royalists." With a characteristic disregard for facts and the meanings of words, they went merrily about their task. Stone, Brandeis, and Cardozo were the heroes of the piece when they voted to uphold New Deal legislation; Van Devanter, McReynolds, Butler, and Sutherland were the villains; Hughes and Roberts were "good guys" when they voted with the liberals and "bad guys" when they voted with the conservatives. Yet the question arose: why did Roosevelt press for the passage of the court-packing scheme in the face of overwhelming opposition from his own party and at a time when the Court seemed to be swinging, partially at least, to his side?

In the case of Roosevelt himself, the answer must lie partly in his overweening egotism. He thought he could get away with anything. But in the case of the socialist revolutionaries who were more and more surrounding the President, the real answer was revealed in the hearings on the court-packing bill in the Senate. Burton K. Wheeler, the Democratic senator who led the fight against the bill, called before the committee only well-known liberals. For weeks, before the senators there paraded authorities on constitutional law, lawyers, educators, writers whose reputations as liberals could not be questioned. There was Raymond Moley, only a short time before a member of Roosevelt's brain trust, Dorothy Thompson, Walter Lippmann, Dr. Harold W. Dodds of Princeton, Dean Young B. Smith of Columbia Law, and many others. *Every one of them had been critical of the Court's anti-New Deal decisions*. But every one of them declared that the Court should not be tampered with. Much as they disagreed with the actions of the Court, they were horrified at the idea of scrapping a free and independent Court and setting up in its place a Court subservient to the unconstitutional aggressions of the Executive.

In the eyes of the socialist revolutionaries who surrounded the President, the men on the Court who might sometimes vote in favor of this or that piece of New Deal legislation were of the same stripe as the witnesses who appeared in opposition to the court-packing bill. They were for reform—but reform *within the American constitutional system*. They could not be trusted to scrap the

Constitution and thus open the way for the establishment of a collectivist state in America. And so a willing President was egged on to carry his fight against the Court to the bitter end.

The Senate's defeat of Roosevelt's court-packing scheme looked to be a stinging defeat for the President— and it was—but Congress unknowingly put into his hands the power he was seeking. It did pass a law permitting Supreme Court justices to retire at 70 on full pay. Weary and disgusted with the attacks on them personally and on the Court generally, two of the older justices, Van Devanter and Sutherland, retired. Time and death did the rest; Cardozo and Butler died and Brandeis resigned. So, in the two years following the defeat of the court-packing plan, Roosevelt was able to fill vacancies on the Court with four new justices—Hugo L. Black, Stanley F. Reed, Felix Frankfurter, and William O. Douglas.

# CHAPTER FIVE

# Court Packing Begins—Black and Reed

Justice Black, at the present writing the oldest member of the Court in point of service, though not in age, is the enigma of the bench. He was born in 1886 in Harlan, Alabama, in a cross-roads cabin in the small-farm country. He was the eighth child in a family supported by a country storekeeper, so his formal schooling was slight. He was largely self-educated until he entered the University of Alabama, where he got his law degree in 1906. As a member of the Senate in the early New Deal days, he went to the limits of congressional power—and beyond—in lashing out at so-called lobbyists. The "lobbyists" were private business interests—the favorite whipping boys of that day—and Senator Black used tactics which made the late Senator McCarthy's attacks on communists seem mild by comparison—a fact conveniently forgotten by McCarthy's enemies.

Black's reputation at the time of his appointment had been made as chairman of Senate committees investigat-

26

ing, first, merchant-marine and air-mail subsidies, and later, the lobbies. In the latter activity he seized from telegraph agencies and private corporations files containing more than five million telegrams and letters in his search for evidence against business interests. This brought down on his head such a storm of public protest that he felt called upon to defend not only himself but the Senate's prerogatives. Attempts to discredit his investigation "by calling it a fishing expedition," he denounced. He declared that a congressional investigation "is not a trial based upon an indictment where the facts are already known and merely need presentation to a jury. It is a study in the public interest."

Twenty years later, when the Supreme Court took it upon itself practically to wipe out the investigating powers of Congress, Justice Black was to join the Court in declaring: ". . . there is no congressional power to expose for the sake of exposure." When Senator Black was out to "get" a businessman or a private corporation, he believed that "most valuable of all, this power of the probe is one of the most powerful weapons in the hands of the people to restrain the activities of powerful groups *who can defy every other power*" (italics added). But Justice Black, faced with the defiant power of the communist conspiracy, declares with the Court that a congressional investigation of an admitted accomplice of communists is "a new kind of congressional inquiry unknown in prior periods of American history." Agents and accomplices of the Red tyranny evidently occupy a much more favorable spot in Justice Black's mind than an American businessman.

Perhaps because of his antipathy to private business, Senator Black became President Roosevelt's first appointee to the Supreme Court, despite the fact that his previous judicial experience consisted of 18 months as a police-court judge. But, for all that, Justice Black had a sharp and busy mind and became one of the hardest-working and most industrious members of the Court.

But a busy mind is not necessarily a straight-thinking mind, particularly when subjected to unexpected pressures. Shortly after Black's appointment, it was revealed that he had once been a member of the Ku Klux Klan. He had already been confirmed by the Senate and had gone off to Europe on a vacation. He returned to find the country seething with speculation as to whether the story was true or not. He went on the air in a nationwide radio address and admitted the charge. But he stayed on the Court. His sharp mind has been busy ever since proving how "liberal" he is. He became known as the leading dissenter on the Court, though in recent years, as the Court has swung more and more to the left and thus closer to Justice Black's philosophy, his dissents have gradually lessened.

Justice Black's own words are the best indication of the contempt in which he holds the American system and its Constitution. In 1955 he declared, "The world could not do better than to follow the political and social ideas" of the late Dr. Albert Einstein. Dr. Einstein may have been a great scientist, but his "political and social" ideas were much more akin to those of Soviet Russia than of the American republic. That, of course, did not deter Dr. Einstein—when he was fleeing Hitler's Germany—from choosing the long journey to the capitalist United States rather than the much shorter one to the socialist heaven to the East. Once here, he exercised his "political and social" ideas, which Justice Black so much admired, by advising young men to treat with disdain the efforts of congressional committees to ferret out communist termites.

Roosevelt's second appointee to the Court, Justice Stanley Reed, was from Kentucky. He was born there in 1884 in Mason County. He got his Bachelor of Arts degree from Kentucky Wesleyan College and later studied law at Columbia and the Universities of Virginia and Paris. But there is no record of his ever receiving a Bachelor of Laws degree. He, too, had no previous judicial experience. He was a Democrat who became a reliable New Deal bureaucrat, though he began his Washington career with the Federal Farm Board under Hoover. As Roosevelt's Solicitor General he argued, and lost, the NRA and AAA cases before the Supreme Court. Before that, he was chief counsel to the Reconstruction Finance Corporation, and it may have been his advice in that post which endeared him to Roosevelt. When a question arose as to the constitutionality of a New Deal measure—the suspension of the gold standard which wiped out contractual obligations calling for payment in gold—Reed evidently advised the Attorney-General that he should take the position that while the act might be unconstitutional, it was all right because it didn't do anybody any harm!

In later years, however, the Court apparently went too far to the left for Justice Reed, and he began to dissent in a number of cases, particularly those involving the communist conspiracy. Perhaps he had finally come to regret the contempt he seemingly felt for the Constitution back in 1937. In that year he made a speech in which he sneered at fixed precedents in law and spoke of the "stagnation of slavish adherence to the past." Unfortunately, that regret—if he felt it—came too late to prevent him from going along with the Court in the most revolutionary decision of recent years, as we shall see.

Justice Reed retired from the Court in 1957. Toward the end of that year, he was named to be the first head of President Eisenhower's extremely controversial Civil Rights Commission. After a few weeks of soul searching, to the surprise and shock of the Eisenhower administration Justice Reed declined the post, declaring it would be improper for him to serve, inasmuch as he was still on call to hear cases in the lower federal courts.

# CHAPTER SIX

# Court Packing Continues—Frankfurter

Next in order on the newly packed Court came Justice Felix Frankfurter, at this writing the oldest member in age. He was the son of Austrian Jewish parents who emigrated to this country in 1894, when Felix was 12 years old, and settled on New York's lower East Side. His family was not well-to-do, but neither was it very poor. Young Felix did odd jobs while attending the New York public schools and later the College of the City of New York. His earnings went into a special fund for his education. On graduation from CCNY—third in his class though he was only 19 years old—he got a civil service job for one year with the New York City Tenement House Commission. He saved almost his entire salary of $1200 and used it to enter Harvard Law School in 1903.

He graduated from Harvard Law in 1906, worked for two months in a Wall Street law firm, and then got a job in the United States Attorney's office for the Southern District of New York. The office was in charge of young

Henry L. Stimson, who had been commissioned by President Theodore Roosevelt to bust some trusts around Manhattan. Stimson needed assistants and asked the dean of Harvard Law School to make recommendations. He recommended Frankfurter, and Stimson hired him. Frankfurter spent the next five years helping Stimson bust trusts. Then, in 1911, when Stimson went to Washington to serve in President Taft's cabinet, he took Frankfurter with him. Many years later, Frankfurter was able to return the favor when he induced Franklin D. Roosevelt to name the aging Stimson, a Republican, as Secretary of War in 1940.

Frankfurter stayed on in Washington after Wilson became President, serving in various minor administration posts and constituting himself a sort of one-man brain trust for his superiors. He came to know Justice Oliver Wendell Holmes, who was one of his two heroes. The other was Louis D. Brandeis, not yet on the Court but already making a name for himself—and compensating for his earlier millionaire law practice—by upholding the rights of the downtrodden against bigness in business. Brandeis was an influential Harvard alumnus and it was he who had Frankfurter appointed to a professorship in the Harvard Law School in 1914. The professor took a leave from Harvard in 1917 to serve his country during wartime—in a civilian post in Washington—but returned to Harvard when the war ended. There he remained until his appointment to the Supreme Court in 1939. It was during his wartime service in Washington that his friendship began with the then Assistant Secretary of the Navy, Franklin D. Roosevelt.

Justice Frankfurter's philosophy is not an easy one to classify, perhaps because he really hasn't any, but suits his views to the exigencies of the moment. That, of course, is any man's right, but the Supreme Court of the United States is hardly a forum for opportunistic "thinking." Justice Frankfurter has been called everything from a communist or socialist to a rank reactionary—not without reason. It would be possible to cite quotations from Frankfurter on every side of every question at one time or another. So slight is his concern with constitutionality and law that he has not only reversed decisions of innumerable preceding courts but has even reversed himself.

In the decision of the Court which so grievously hamstrings the power of congressional investigation, Frankfurter went out of his way to write a concurring opinion in which he said that questions put to a witness "must be defined with sufficient unambiguous clarity to safeguard a witness from the hazards of vagueness . . ." How very different from an earlier dictum from the pen of Mr. Frankfurter when he was a professor at Harvard Law School. Then he declared: "The power of investigation should be left untrammeled, and the methods and forms of each investigation should be left to Congress and its committees, as each situation arises."

Frankfurter once wrote a book about labor injunctions (*The Labor Injunction*). He was against them. But in 1940 he wrote an opinion *upholding* an injunction against a Chicago labor union which prohibited any of its members from peaceful picketing. Did this mean that Justice Frankfurter had finally made up his mind where he stood on labor problems? Not at all, for in 1956 he concurred in an opinion of the Court ordering three railway employees to join a union if they wanted to keep their jobs.

Frankfurter's variable principles have been evident on the Court on more than one occasion. The Court once had before it the case of a religious sect—Jehovah's Witnesses. Some of its members had been convicted in New Haven, Conn., for making speeches and passing out literature attacking the Catholic Church. The Supreme Court—with Justice Frankfurter concurring—reversed the conviction on the ground that it was an interference with freedom of speech and religion. A few years later the same sect was before the Court again because several children of its members had refused to salute the flag (in accordance with their religious beliefs). This time, to everyone's amazement, Justice Frankfurter wrote the majority opinion upholding conviction by a lower court, which led one of the Justice's former admirers to remark that Frankfurter was "heroically saving America from a couple of school children." Justice Stone, in a vigorous dissent, confronted Justice Frankfurter with his own words and arguments, but there was no evident discomfiture on Frankfurter's part. The question here is not when Justice Frankfurter was right and when he was wrong. The point is that he himself does not seem to know.

Justice Frankfurter cannot be classified as either a communist, a socialist, a conservative or a reactionary. He has been called power-mad. But he was not power-mad in the sense that he wanted to hold sway over great masses of people. His power hunger expressed itself more in the Machiavellian sense, in a need to sit behind the scenes and manipulate the men and events on the public stage. It has perhaps been best expressed by a very friendly critic, Matthew Josephson. Some of Frankfurter's friends felt he should not take the Supreme Court post because he already had a much bigger position. Josephson said (*New Yorker,* Nov. 30, 1940):

It was a very high position, although one that was nowhere described in the Constitution. He was a whole institution in himself. He was an Influence, a prodigious and pervasive one, working upon men and situations in every part of the country . . . Perhaps most important, he was, some well-posted observers believed, a Jiminy Cricket to President Roosevelt's Pinocchio —Jiminy Cricket, the chirping little Keeper of the Conscience, always worrying about the scrapes Pinocchio might get into, always turning up with advice when he was in trouble, but always . . . beautifully devoted to his big, happy-go-lucky, venturesome friend and master.

It is essential for one who would practice this Machiavellian art in the muddy waters of public life that he should not have too fundamental a set of convictions— constitutional or otherwise. The overpowering motivation of Frankfurter's life is a desire to pull strings. He would have made a marvelous puppeteer. He had discovered, long before his friend Roosevelt became president, that a professor of law at Harvard could have widespread influence. A letter from him—on the stationery of the Harvard Law School—opened and closed doors as if by magic. Once his friend was in the White House, the vista before him must have seemed boundless. During his 25 years at Harvard—where, as one colleague put it, "he teaches Felix Frankfurter, not law"—he had at his disposal the malleable minds of hundreds of American youths. Before, and especially after, the advent of the New Deal, when he found himself able to place many of his pets in sensitive Washington jobs, he was in his glory. Two of his very special ones were Alger Hiss and Dean Acheson. In Frankfurter's case "the evil that men do" will not only live after him; it survives notoriously in the China debacle over which Dean Acheson presided and in the spectacle of an American perjurer sitting at President Roosevelt's elbow at the infamous Yalta Conference.

Washington swarmed with scores of Frankfurter's pets. In addition to Acheson and Hiss, there were Tommy Corcoran, Ben Cohen, Archibald MacLeish and James M. Landis, to name a few of the better known. It has been estimated that at least 300 of Frankfurter's former students found their way into strategic spots in Washington bureaus through the intervention of their professor. They were Frankfurter's "boys"—the "happy hot dogs" —and through them he was molding the policies of a nation. So heady a drug was not one to be lightly relinquished by a man of Frankfurter's turn of mind. Roosevelt sprang his court-packing plan while Frankfurter was still at Harvard, though making frequent weekly trips to Washington. He was opposed to the plan—so much so that he actually became ill while the assault on the Court was in progress. But Roosevelt had it in his power to cut the strings by which Frankfurter controlled his pup-

pets. A man with strong convictions about American constitutional law could hardly have remained quiet in the
face of the President's daring attack on the Court. But
Felix Frankfurter managed to stay silent.

Not long after, despite a total lack of judicial experience, or even any experience in the practice of law, he
got his reward in an appointment to the Supreme Court.
Roosevelt had offered him the Solicitor-Generalship in
1933, but Frankfurter had turned it down—he had his
eye on higher stakes. In fact, Roosevelt had wanted to
make him Solicitor-General even earlier, when he was
forming his original team. The redoubtable Tom Walsh,
Roosevelt's first Attorney-General who died before he
could take office, refused to have Frankfurter as his
Solicitor-General. Walsh said he didn't want someone
"who would lose cases in the grand manner."

After he had joined the High Court, Frankfurter's
string pulling became more effective than ever. He restored Dean Acheson to the good graces of the administration, after Acheson had left the New Deal in its early
days in a disagreement over monetary policy. It was
Frankfurter, according to former Secretary of the Treasury Henry Morgenthau, Jr., who had Acheson named
Assistant Secretary of State. Acheson would one day become Secretary of State—and refuse to turn his back on
Alger Hiss. And Justice Frankfurter would turn up as a
character witness for Hiss at his first trial and go out of
his way to shake the hand of the perjurer for all to see.
Hiss had been one of "his boys."

The Justice is a man who talks about everything and
anything—and when he talks, he brooks no interference

from lesser minds. Even FDR once said that Felix gave him mental indigestion. And Frankfurter himself will occasionally tell of the time his host apologized for the noise at a Washington soirée. The Justice replied: "Noise? Why, I like noise." Whereupon Mrs. Frankfurter broke in: "Yes, dear, but this is other people's noise."

It finally took the sharp-tongued daughter of Theodore Roosevelt—Mrs. Alice Roosevelt Longworth—to stop Frankfurter in the midst of one of his dissertations at a Washington dinner party. In a defense of his protégé Acheson, he was busily engaged in a tirade on the administrative and military misdeeds of General Douglas MacArthur. Mrs. Longworth, failing in all attempts to correct Frankfurter's statements, finally rose, left the table— and the room—with one parting shot: "I refuse to turn my back on General MacArthur."

Justice Frankfurter could speak sneeringly of MacArthur. But, several years later, atom spies Julius and Ethel Rosenberg asked the Court for a stay of execution. A majority of the Court refused to grant it—but Justice Frankfurter joined Justices Black and Douglas in dissenting.

# CHAPTER SEVEN

# And Goes On—Douglas

If Justice Black is an enigma, and Justice Frankfurter's slippery slide back and forth across the bench makes it difficult for us to tag him, at least no such uncertainty surrounds Roosevelt's fourth appointment to the Court —that of Justice William O. Douglas. He was born in Maine, Minnesota, in 1898, but grew up in near poverty with his widowed mother in Yakima, Washington. He had polio as a boy. It affected both legs and caused him to concentrate on books. His subsequent recovery he attributes to tramping the foothills of the Cascade Mountains near his home in Yakima. Douglas worked his way through Whitman College at Walla Walla. He wanted to come East to get his law degree, but had no money. A job tending a shipment of sheep got him to Minnesota. From there he rode the freights to Chicago and then borrowed the train fare to New York. Part-time teaching at Columbia and a job in a law firm enabled him to get his law degree. He went back to Yakima to practice, but Columbia offered him a full-time teaching job. From there he went to Yale, where he became a professor of law. Like many other professors of that day, he wound up in Washington with a government job in the Securities Exchange Commission, of which he later became chairman.

Justice Douglas is an out-and-out leftist—the darling of the radicals. He is also something of a publicity seeker who has broken all precedents in conduct of Supreme Court justices by engaging in partisan debate outside the Court.

It may be that his yen for public notice—as evidenced by sojourns to Russia, a 189-mile hike in Maryland decked out in a Western-style hat, being thrown by a yak in Kashmir (these and other adventures generally resulting in magazine articles and books)—stems from disappointment at once having had the presidency of the United States almost within his grasp, only to see it slip from him because he was too left even for the leftists.

Douglas had the whole left-wing faction of the Democratic Party behind him for the vice-presidential nomination at the 1944 convention. That was the convention at which Henry Wallace was dumped. It was also the convention at which the vice-presidential nomination was tantamount to the presidency, since the insiders doubted that Roosevelt had long to live. Douglas was Roosevelt's personal choice for the nomination, as the Justice well knew. He was at a remote fishing camp in Oregon, waiting for the "call." But the professional politicians in Chicago had other ideas. They couldn't see themselves swallowing Douglas's radicalism after having just got rid of

Wallace. So Harry Truman got the nomination—and the presidency—and Douglas stayed on the Supreme Court.

Not once—either before or since that incident—has Douglas deviated from the left-wing position in any case involving the communist conspiracy that has come before the Court. One of his oddest acts—and one that very nearly resulted in impeachment proceedings against him—was the order staying the execution of the Rosenbergs. It was a fantastic performance—and seemingly a meaningless one. The Supreme Court on four separate occasions had refused to consider any further legal moves by the Rosenbergs' attorneys. His action—taken alone while the Court was not in session—accomplished nothing save to give the atom spies a few more days among the living. As soon as Chief Justice Vinson could convene the full Court, it acted immediately to reverse Justice Douglas's lone-wolf gesture—with Messrs. Douglas, Frankfurter, and Black dissenting—and the Rosenbergs went to their deaths.

Why, then, did Douglas make the gesture? He, himself, of course, put it on the high ground of the law without thus seeming to commit himself to the loud and blatant defenders of the Rosenbergs. But there are those who believe that Douglas has never quite got over being within a breath of the domicile at the other end of Pennsylvania Avenue. He is comparatively young, as Supreme Court justices go, and some of those "in the know" think he is banking on a wave of the not-too-distant future when the legions of the far left will be in the saddle and looking about for a presidential candidate. To these observers, Douglas—in the Rosenberg case as in many others—is simply building up for himself an annuity that will insure the dreamed-of mantle falling where it belongs—on his shoulders.

Whether this be true or not, the fact remains that Justice Douglas has gone outside the Court to plug for the admission of Red China to the United Nations and for American recognition of Red China. He has told a Sarah Lawrence College audience—*after* many of the exposures of native Reds and of what they had done to us and the world—that "an awful thing happened when the politicians decided to vie with each other in denouncing communism." He wants the United Nations charter amended to permit the formation of a world government, and he has accepted a one-thousand-dollar award from the left-wing Sidney Hillman Foundation. On that occasion Douglas sang a paean of praise for the deceased Hillman, the labor leader who used goons and gangsters like Louis Lepke as the "enforcement" machinery for his leftist aims.

Justice Douglas makes speeches before CIO conventions. His horror at bigness in business does not seem to extend to bigness in labor. He told one CIO convention that labor should get into the international field, take over the job of the diplomats and become America's ambassadors to a "new Europe." Heaven knows, many of our State Department representatives abroad have not always been to our liking, to put it mildly. But picture, if you can, a diplomatic corps made up of Dave Beck, James Hoffa, Jimmy Petrillo, Mike Quill, *et al.!*

Justice Douglas also thinks Moscow-loving Nehru of India is "not a dangerous man but a great bulwark against communism." He goes out of his way to stay in the good graces of the Russians. On one of his numerous trips, when he criticized the Soviet Asiatic republics as colonies of Russia, *Pravda* jumped on him, whereupon he took occasion to praise the cultural achievements of Asiatic Russia. At a press conference in Washington to which only Russian reporters were admitted—while the American press representatives cooled their heels outside his office—Douglas said he was very impressed by the progress he found among Russian courts, lawyers, and judges. No doubt this pronouncement, cabled to Russia as the statement of a justice of the Supreme Court of the United States, provided cooling balm for those Russians who had seen their relatives and friends executed or banished to Siberia by those same courts and judges.

Douglas, too, had had no previous judicial experience when named to the Court. And so it was easy for him to tell another audience at Occidental College in 1949 that the only answer to communism was the Welfare State, with much less emphasis on property rights. However, pending the arrival of this propertyless state, which will "answer communism" by bringing it to power, the Justice keeps an anchor to windward. He was the only Washington official who attended the annual reception at the Soviet Embassy in 1956. Anger over Soviet action in putting down the Hungarian revolt was at its height and every important Western official stayed away. Douglas felt called upon to answer the storm of criticism which came down on him and said he didn't know the reception was being boycotted. A year later, the Reds held another reception to celebrate the 40th anniversary of the Russian revolution. Once again, there was Justice Douglas; which led the *National Review* to ask if he had ever left the Soviet Embassy.

# CHAPTER EIGHT

# *And on—Murphy and Rutledge*

President Roosevelt made four more appointments to the Supreme Court before his death in 1945—Justices Murphy, Byrnes, Jackson, and Rutledge. Justice James F. Byrnes was a former congressman and senator from South Carolina. He served on the Court for only one year. He resigned to fill several important wartime posts under Roosevelt, later became Truman's Secretary of State, and still later Governor of South Carolina. In recent years he has become one of the Court's severest critics and his words carry much weight since, as a former justice, he knows whereof he speaks.

Justice Robert H. Jackson, we will consider later, together with those other members of the Court who rendered the decision which promises to keep America torn by racial dissension for years to come.

Justice Frank Murphy was still another of the Roosevelt appointees to the Court who had had no previous judicial experience, unless one counts a stint as judge of the Recorders' Court in Detroit. Murphy, son of poor immigrant parents, typified the old-time novelist's conception of the "fighting Irishman," though his battles were not with his fists. He was born (in 1890) and raised in Michigan, and got his education and his law degree at the University of Michigan. Murphy made himself champion of the so-called "underdog" and, in the process, developed a mystical belief in the soaring star of his own destiny. This belief did not preclude even the presidency of the United States, and he once asked a companion plaintively if he didn't think it was possible for a Catholic to be elected.

Murphy became the "poor man's" Mayor of Detroit at the bottom of the depression—just prior to Roosevelt's first campaign for the presidency. The Mayor's sympathy extended to the "underprivileged" of all classes. He made Mrs. Eleanor Roosevelt's hapless brother, Hall Roosevelt, City Comptroller of Detroit. His reward came in the form of appointment by Roosevelt to be Governor-General and then High Commissioner of the Philippines. From that post he was called home by the New Deal politicos to run for Governor of Michigan. During his tenure as governor of that state, one of the most disgraceful episodes in American industrial history took place within Murphy's jurisdiction, while the "fighting Irishman" sat quietly—and inactively—in the executive mansion at Lansing.

On New Year's Day, 1937, a strike was called in the great automobile plants of Michigan. Twenty-six thousand men quit work in the General Motors plants. Within the next ten days, 135,000 workers were on strike. But this was no ordinary strike, in which workers, exercising their right to collective bargaining, walked out of the plants and refused to carry on production until their terms were met by the employers, or a compromise reached—at which time they would return to the plants. The workers —or a good number of them—*seized the plants*. Two weeks after the strike was called, the largest plants in the automobile industry in Michigan—built, maintained, financed, and managed by American private enterprise —were in the hands of the "sit-down" strikers inside the plants.

The famous Michigan sit-down strike was instigated, organized, and carried out by the communists. No less an authority than Benjamin Gitlow, a former communist who once headed the Communist Party in the United States, said in 1948 (in his book *The Whole of Their Lives*):

> The Detroit district of the Communist party holds a unique position in the Communist party organization. Since 1929, the ablest Party organizers have been put in charge of its affairs. . . . In the Detroit district are also to be found some of the oldest and most capable Communist trade union officials and Party organizers, men and women who have been purposely sent there from other districts.

Gitlow pointed out that in the sit-down strikes the communists were trying out a new technique in industrial warfare. They "seized factories by staging sit-down strikes. The country was treated to a preview of things to come, of how the communists intended to seize the factories by occupying them from the inside and converting each factory into a fortress of the Communist revolution."

The sit-down strikes aroused a country that was generally sympathetic to the aims of labor. What many people could not understand was why the governor of a sovereign American state should sit by and allow the illegal seizure of private property within his state without lifting a finger. Bascom N. Timmons reported (in *Garner of Texas*) that Vice President Garner went to the President to point out the constitutional issue involved. The Constitution guarantees to each state a republican form of government. Roosevelt admitted he believed the sit-down strikes were illegal. Garner wanted him to say so publicly in the hope it would force Murphy, who owed his election to Roosevelt, to act to preserve republican government in Michigan. Roosevelt refused to make a statement, which brought from the angry Garner the retort that the labor leaders had become bigger men than the President.

The following year, Frank Murphy was defeated for reelection as Governor of Michigan. But this would not shake belief in his star of destiny, because Roosevelt brought him to Washington and made him Attorney-General of the United States. He was welcomed with open arms by the Washington gossip columnists. He was a bachelor who enjoyed squiring pretty women around Washington. He was a convivial party-goer who never took a drink. He had a temper that went well with his red hair. And this "poor man's friend" and battler for the underprivileged found his bosom pals among the richest of Washington's society.

Murphy served only twelve months as Attorney-General, during which he went after some of the sacred cows of the Democratic Party. He started prosecutions against Tom Pendergast and sent Moe Annenberg to prison. That star of destiny must have been twinkling very brightly in his mind's eye, what with the 1940 presidential nominations coming up. But he reckoned without his mentor. There were rumors that Murphy was going to go after Ed Kelly, who controlled the Democratic machine in Chicago, and Frank Hague, who did the same in Jersey City. Roosevelt needed Boss Kelly and Boss Hague to swing a third-term nomination for himself.

In any case, in 1940 Roosevelt named Murphy to a vacancy on the Supreme Court created by the death of Pierce Butler. Familiar with Murphy's mercurially unjudicious temperament, some wag was led to remark that we would now have "justice tempered with Murphy." It probably never will be known whether Murphy was elevated to the Court because he was a Catholic (as was Butler), or to remove him from the Justice Department, where he was said thoroughly to have messed up its administrative machinery, or to get him off the necks of Bosses Kelly and Hague. The last explanation seems the most logical.

Once on the Court, Murphy continued his gay life in Washington and among New York's "café society." This evidently left him little time for the work of the Court, because he wrote few decisions. He seemed to have little liking for the quiet, secluded atmosphere of the Court and no doubt missed sorely the life of active politics. But, in the Court's decisions, he invariably followed the lead of Frankfurter. Prior to some feuding—of which more later —that developed among the justices, Frankfurter had Murphy's vote in every case but one. Generally Murphy could be found in the same "judicial" camp as Frankfurter, Black, and Douglas. He died in 1949, as the result of a heart condition from which he had suffered for some time. However, there are those who believe that what really killed him was the realization that his star had finally flickered out. The Supreme Court post seemed to be about as far as he could go—and that was not what the star had promised. He was in many ways a tragic figure, because he undoubtedly believed implicitly in the New Deal, to which he gave his undying loyalty. His only reward was to be kicked upstairs to a post for which he was totally unfitted.

Roosevelt's last appointee to the Court—Justice Wiley B. Rutledge—was the first to have had any judicial experience worth mentioning. He was born in Cloverport, Kentucky, in 1894, but went to the University of Wisconsin. He taught school in Indiana, New Mexico, and Colorado, and then, in 1922, got his law degree at the University of Colorado. He served successively as professor of law and then dean of the law school at Washington University. His next job was at the State University of Iowa. From there he had come to Washington in 1939 to serve on the United States Court of Appeals for the District of Columbia—an appointment which was a reward for his thorough New Dealism while he was

Dean of the Law School of the State University of Iowa. He had been wholeheartedly for Roosevelt's court-packing scheme and, when the four conservatives on the High Court did not act to Professor Rutledge's liking, he cynically remarked that the "Four Horsemen do not know that we had an election." Presumably his belief that the Court should decide cases not according to the Constitution but according to the election returns earned him his elevation to the highest court in 1943. He died in 1949, so that his tenure on the Court was relatively brief. But it was long enough for the leftists to take him to their hearts, since he voted in 98 percent of the cases with their heroes—Douglas, Black, and Murphy.

# CHAPTER NINE

# Up and Down Is Across—the Elevator Decision

By the time America entered the Second World War in 1941, there remained on the Supreme Court only two judges who had not been named by President Roosevelt. They were Justices Stone and Roberts—and Justice Stone owed his appointment as Chief Justice to the President. In the pre-war and war years this packed Court proceeded to perform a major operation on the Constitution of the United States by removing many of its vital organs. Succeeding justices named by President Truman, and particularly by President Eisenhower, about completed the job—so much so that we might say that the body of the Constitution remains, but only as a mere shell, devoid of arteries, veins, heart, and lungs. And in the manner of quack medicine men, they performed the operation without the permission of either the patient or his guardians.

There is only one legal way in which the Constitution can be changed—by amendment initiated by the sovereign states or by the Congress and concurred in by *three fourths of the states.* These nine judges simply usurped the powers of the states and the people's representatives and tore to pieces the charter of freedom of the American people.

In farming and agriculture, the Court made possible that myriad of bureaus and bureaucrats which has nearly returned the once free and independent American farmer to European serfdom. Only, now, the serfdom is to an all-pervading and all-powerful central government instead of to individual autocratic barons. The Court has made possible the fantastic circus of the past decade and a half in which billions of dollars are taken from American taxpayers and paid to farmers in order to keep prices of farm products high to those same taxpayers. And we have had the almost obscene spectacle in the "land of the free" of a farmer being forced to pay a fine to the federal bureaucrats because he raised some extra wheat—over and above the decreed quota—to feed to his own hogs or to grind into flour for his own bread. A single example, among many, is that of Dr. P. S. Whiteleather, a Minerva, Ohio, physician who owns a 150-acre farm. He was fined $450 for overplanting his wheat allotment in 1954. The government has been trying to collect the fine ever since, but Dr. Whiteleather, in 1957, declared it would have to foreclose on his $25,000 farm to collect the penalty. Other farmers, wanting to hold onto their land, pay up meekly.

In industry, with the blessing of the Court, the federal bureaucrats swarm over what was once known as "free enterprise," tell it whom, when, where and how to hire and fire and for what it must sell its products. And over the American worker (we must admit, in many instances with his acquiescence) the Court has placed the heavy and often corrupt hand of the politically minded labor leader—a process which brings us up against a union monopoly much more terrifying, because of the numbers and funds involved, than the old trust monopolies against which modern-day "liberals" still inveigh.

With the appointment of the new judges by President Roosevelt from 1937 on, the socialist revolutionaries in America had what they needed—a Supreme Court which would ignore the rights of the states and set up the central government in Washington as the all-powerful element in American life.

The justices went about their demolition job on the Constitution in the manner characteristic of our social revolutionaries of the past twenty years. They simply changed the meaning of a few words and phrases whose true intent had been thoroughly understood—and interpreted—by Supreme Courts for 148 years. The diabolical cunning involved in this usurpation by the judges of the rights of states and citizens is easily illustrated.

The destruction of the rights of the states was the primary objective because, as we have pointed out, in no other way could a collectivist society be imposed on America. In 1942, in the midst of our first year of fighting in the Second World War, when nobody was paying much attention to the Supreme Court, Justice Frankfurter struck a major blow for the Constitution wreckers. He did it by twisting out of all recognition one little phrase in the Constitution which gives the federal government power over "interstate commerce." The Constitution left in the hands of the sovereign states all powers of regulation over their internal trade, business, and commercial operations. But it recognized that when citizens of one state traded with citizens of another state, the only possible regulatory body could be the Congress in Washington. And so it gave Congress the right to regulate trade which *crossed state lines.* That trade, and that alone, came within the regulatory power of the federal government, and it had been so held by innumerable Supreme Courts.

But this did not suit Justice Frankfurter and his revolutionary cohorts on the court. He cooked up a brand-new decision (A.B. Kirschbaum v. Walling)—with no precedent in law or fact—by which the federal government might intrude into purely state functions. One of the tenants of a loft building in a New Jersey town was a clothing manufacturer who sold most of his products in other states. He was, clearly, in interstate commerce and thus subject to federal regulation.

But Justice Frankfurter declared that the building— inside a town inside the sovereign state of New Jersey— was also engaged in interstate commerce because that one tenant, among many others, was engaged in interstate commerce. And that wasn't all. By means of his judicial "reasoning," Justice Frankfurter went further, saying that, because the building was in interstate commerce, *so was the elevator man who ran the elevator up and down in the building,* and the women who washed the windows!

If you, a small businessman—or you, a worker in an industry within a state—or you, just an average citizen going about your daily duties—ever wonder how it has come about that the reaching arm of the Washington politician has come to rest so heavily on all your activities, there is your answer, supplied by Justice Frankfurter.

# CHAPTER TEN

# "Civil Liberties"—for Whom?

This was the "liberal" Supreme Court which was supposed to have struck such great blows for what is known by that much-abused phrase "civil liberties." It was the Roosevelt Court's actions—as well as those of the Court of today—in this field which brought, and still brings, great gladness to all the bleedings hearts of the brave new (collectivist) world. But "civil liberties" for whom?

In 1943, a case came before the packed Court involving one William Schneiderman. He was a member of the Communist Party. He was not a native American. He had applied for citizenship and was granted his naturalization certificate. Then it came to the attention of the immigration authorities that he was a communist and had been one when he got his citizenship papers. The government rescinded his naturalization on the ground that he had not taken the oath of allegiance to the United States in good faith. A communist, of course, cannot possibly swear allegiance to the United States in good faith, since his only allegiance is to the communist conspiracy. Schneiderman took the case (Schneiderman v. U.S.) to the Supreme Court, which magnanimously gave him back his citizenship on the ground that, once conferred, citizenship could not be taken away.

Another case (Bridges v. Wixon) involved a notorious alien—Harry Bridges—who came here from Australia and became a powerful West Coast labor leader whose longshoremen's union was rank with communism. Bridges was prosecuted under the Alien Registration Act, in which Congress declared that any alien who, at the time he came to this country or later, was a member of, or was affiliated with, an organization advocating the forceful overthrow of the government could be deported —sent back to the country from which he came. The prosecution showed that Bridges had worked closely with the Communist Party and had supported its political candidates. But the Supreme Court of the United States, speaking through Justice Douglas, declared this did not constitute "affiliation"—and Bridges stayed.

Bridges finally applied for citizenship—and got it. But it subsequently developed that he had lied in the deportation proceedings which ended with his getting a clean bill of health from the Supreme Court. He was tried, convicted of perjury, and given a jail sentence—and his naturalization was canceled. Once again he appealed to the Supreme Court. And once again the Court freed him—not because he wasn't guilty, but because the statute of limitations had run out.

So Harry Bridges is still amongst us—a monument to the defense of "civil liberties" by the Supreme Court.

That's how our "liberal" Supreme Court handled the case of a naturalized communist citizen and an alien, left-wing labor leader. But let us see what happened in the case of not one or two but *120,000 native-born American citizens.* This case, and the two mentioned above, all occurred during the Second World War, so it is no excuse to say that the Court must take into consideration the exigencies of wartime.

These 120,000 people were Americans of Japanese descent who lived on the West Coast. Their crime was that they had the same color skin as did the people of a nation with whom we were at war. No doubt there were some traitors amongst them, as there were amongst our German and Italian citizens; and as there were traitors in much greater number working in the interest of our great and noble ally—for the moment—Soviet Russia. But the majority of the Japanese-Americans on the West Coast were loyal American citizens, as was proved by their exemplary behavior under the most trying conditions and the excellent record chalked up by their young men in our armed services.

But President Roosevelt, the patron saint of American "civil liberties," established a special bureau, the War Relocation Authority, which rounded up all 120,000 of these citizens, routed them from their homes, their farms, and their businesses on the West Coast and impounded them in camps in the interior of the country. He called the camps War Relocation Centers. We were more plainspoken in referring to the same type of centers in Europe —we called them concentration camps. *And Roosevelt did this against the explicit advice of J. Edgar Hoover, head of the FBI.* No one knew better than Hoover the importance of national security in wartime; but he wrote the Attorney-General and the President to call attention to the crime they were committing against American civil liberties. Hoover said the whole operation was based not on public interest but on political pressure and hysteria.

In good time a case involving the constitutionality of this mass uprooting of American citizens came before the Supreme Court. And the Court, which wouldn't take citizenship from a foreign-born communist or deport an alien, left-wing labor leader, upheld the concentration-camp impounding of thousands of American citizens. The decision (Korematsu v. U.S.) was written by the leftists' pet defender of "civil liberties"—Justice Black.

This was perhaps the greatest assault on real civil liberties in our history—for, if the President could do what he did to citizens of Japanese ancestry, a President can do it to citizens of German, Italian, Swedish, English, Irish, or any other ancestry, whenever the federal government sees fit to create the occasion. An interesting footnote to this mass assault on civil liberties is provided in the fact that Mr. Roosevelt had the assistance of the then Attorney-General of California—now Chief Justice of the United States, Earl Warren. And the man who headed the so-called War Relocation Authority was Mr. Milton Eisenhower, brother and chief adviser of the President who gave Mr. Warren his Supreme Court post. Between 50 and 60 percent of these displaced Americans of Japanese descent returned to the West Coast states after the war. But they had to start over again from scratch. Congress subsequently voted some money restitution to them, but tenant farmers who had to give up their leases and small-business men who had to close their shops did not get them back. And there is no record that the then Governor of California, Earl Warren —now so solicitous of the "civil rights" of communists— bothered his head about the rights of these native Americans when they returned to his state.

# CHAPTER ELEVEN

# *Truman Names a Chief Justice—Fred M. Vinson*

One decision continued to follow another from the packed Court, each of them designed to break down further the constitutional bars against growing usurpations by the Washington government. The remaining years of the Roosevelt regime and those of the Truman "Fair Deal" saw generally a continuation of the same type of Supreme Court appointments and, with one or two exceptions, the same type of major decisions.

President Truman made four appointments to the Supreme Court—Justice Burton, Chief Justice Vinson, Justices Clark and Minton. Burton, Clark, and Minton we will consider a little later. Fred M. Vinson was named Chief Justice in 1946 to replace Harlan F. Stone. He was Truman's Secretary of the Treasury at the time he was named to the Court. He had been elected to Congress seven times from Kentucky and had held high wartime posts under Roosevelt and Truman. In the interval between his congressional service and his job as Director of

Economic Stabilization, he had gained some judicial experience, from 1938 to 1943, as a member of the Court of Appeals for the District of Columbia. But that was not Truman's main reason for making him Chief Justice. Vinson was named to see if he couldn't bring some order and dignity out of the dissension, petty bickering, and snarling among the justices, which had already broken out in the press.

At the time of Vinson's appointment, with the exception of one earlier Truman appointee, Justice Burton, every member of the Supreme Court had received his appointment at the hands of Franklin Roosevelt. They were all pretty much in the same ideological camp—the left. Of course the gradations ranged from pale pink, right across to just this side of deep red. One would have supposed that such ideological "liberals," now ensconced in the rarefied judicial atmosphere of the Court, with the power in their hands to make or break a great republic, at least could have handled smoothly their personal relations with each other. Somewhere the gods must be laughing at the spectacle of men who would like to see all America become one great state-controlled mass and then fit her neatly into a beautiful collectivist world—at the spectacle of such men being unable to get along with each other. After all, there were only nine of them—nine out of the two and one half billion people to be poured into one great mold.

Justices Jackson and Black were having a feud—which we will go into a little more fully later. Justice Frankfurter disapproved of Justice Murphy's night-clubbing. Justice Douglas and Justice Frankfurter were making sneering remarks about each other. Justice Reed couldn't always be kept in line by Justice Frankfurter, who one day, through the open door of his office, could be heard on the telephone saying to Justice Reed: "Now, Stanley, don't let your vote be influenced by those b - - - - - - s."

Fred Vinson was known as a great compromiser. He was also a congenial and jovial man with a highly developed sense of humor. It was evidently Truman's hope that he would have a tranquilizing influence on the Court and at least quiet some of the Court's household rows that were seeping into the press. By the time he died in 1953, a calm seemed to have settled on the Court. Whether this was due to Vinson's influence, or whether the protagonists, as they grew older, also grew less contentious, is not known.

Vinson, of course, was a New Dealer, though not quite so rabid a variety as Douglas, Black, and Murphy. On the Court he sometimes voted with these leaders of the far "liberal" wing and sometimes with the not-so-far "liberal" group made up of Jackson, Burton, and Reed— and occasionally of Frankfurter, who was busy applying a slippery polish to the bench in his slides from one side to the other.

Toward the end of the Truman regime, it became the fashion among "liberals" to bemoan the "change" in the Court from the great days of the Roosevelt justices. The inconsistency involved here, since the majority of the justices were still Roosevelt appointees, did not bother the "liberals." Their disappointment stemmed chiefly from the fact that the Court as a whole wasn't moving fast enough to the far left to suit them and that, in a few decisions, it actually seemed to be moving back a little toward the Constitution. The "liberals"—never ones for being particular about their use of words—began calling Vinson, Reed, and Minton conservatives and even reactionaries. Minton was a New Deal wheel-horse, as we shall see later, and he, Reed and Vinson were just as good New Dealers as the rest.

Then, in 1952, the "liberals" were set back on their heels—only momentarily, of course—by a decision in which the "liberal" justices seemed to give them a slap in the face and in which they found the "reactionaries," Vinson, Reed, and Minton, on their side. This was the famous case in which a majority of the Court invalidated Harry Truman's seizure of the steel mills.

The United Steelworkers Union of the CIO, then headed by Philip Murray, threatened to strike the steel industry while the Korean War was still in progress. Steel production would have come to a standstill. The President, because of his dislike of the Taft-Hartley Act, refused to invoke one of its provisions which would have kept the steelworkers in the mills for a period of 80 days while a fact-finding board investigated their wage dispute with the employers. Instead, in April, Truman seized the steel mills in the name of the government. The steel companies challenged this high-handed action and District Judge David A. Pine issued an order directing Truman to give the mills back to their rightful owners. The case reached the Supreme Court with unusual speed and in

June, by a six-to-three decision, the Court upheld Pine's order. The union immediately called the men out on strike.

The country had been aroused not only by President Truman's autocratic act in seizing the mills, but also by the unpatriotic attitude of the steelworkers' union—or the union bosses—in threatening to strike a vital industry while the country was at war. For the moment, it looked to the general public as though the Supreme Court was at long last returning to its historic function in protecting the people and the states against unconstitutional seizures of power.

Justice Hugo Black wrote the majority decision for the Court. His words—which gave momentary encouragement to those praying for the return of constitutional government in America—have a strange and hollow sound today in view of subsequent actions of a Court on which Justice Black remained a leading figure. He declared that President Truman had violated the Constitution by *usurping the legislative powers reserved to Congress*. And he said: "The Constitution did not subject this law-making power of Congress to Presidential or military supervision or control." Justice Black and his concurring colleagues have conveniently short memories. If only he and they could have remembered his words two brief years later, when they rendered a decision in which the *Court* usurped the legislative powers reserved to the Congress!

In the jubilation over this seeming proof that in America the law was still greater than the President, it was overlooked that the five concurring justices each went to the unusual length of writing his own concurring opinion. As Arthur Krock (New York *Times,* June 8, 1952) pointed out some days later—when the decision had been all but forgotten in the battle between the striking steelworkers and the employers—these concurring opinions did not close the door to future drastic presidential action taken without a specific law of Congress in unforeseen crises. They also left the door open in the future for the seizure of individual plants—maybe one after another—on a sort of temporary basis until the President could get Congress to approve or regulate his action—or disapprove it. It seems the mistake Harry Truman made was in seizing the steel industry all at once—he should have grabbed one company at a time!

Of particular interest, however, was Chief Justice Vinson's dissent in the steel case. He, together with Justices Reed and Minton, upheld Truman's right to seize the mills. And, as coming events cast their shadow before, we would do well to ponder the Chief Justice's reasoning in this case. We were at war in Korea. But this was not a United States war, the Chief Justice said (although we supplied all the funds, all the matériel, and most of the men). It was a United *Nations* war. We were a member of the United Nations. We, the United States, had an obligation to carry out United Nations mandates. Therefore the United States—just one cog in the great United Nations wheel—was obliged to do anything necessary to the prosecution of the United Nations war in Korea. Therefore, the President had a right to seize the steel mills in order to fulfill our obligation to the United Nations. Disentangled from its legal obfuscations, that was Chief Justice Vinson's reasoning.

Of course, what had really happened in the steel case was that, once again, the Supreme Court had been reading the newspapers—much more carefully than the general public. And even the "liberals" could have saved themselves their momentary dismay over the seeming about-face of their heroes on the Court if they had watched the congressional news a little more closely. Pending before the Armed Services Committee of the House was a bill sponsored by Representative Howard W. Smith of Virginia covering strikes in defense plants. As well as providing for government seizure of mills and industries, *it called for seizure of labor unions.* Following the Court's decision in the steel case, the bill was forgotten.

# CHAPTER TWELVE

# Two Major Bastions

Generally speaking, despite the decision in the steel case, the Roosevelt-Truman Court continued on its way. Even Dr. Carl Brent Swisher, by no means unfriendly to the Court's "liberal" trend, has said (in his book *American Constitutional Development*) that "No New Deal or wartime regulation of economic matters was deemed too extreme to fit into the pattern of the Constitution." And, in a classic of professorial understatement, he remarked: "Because of the individualism of the newly appointed justices and *their lack of traditional reverence for settled law and for the Court itself,* the disturbance during this period was particularly great" (italics added).

As Dwight D. Eisenhower took office in 1953, the sovereign American states and their citizens had become bound up in the ropes of federal authoritarianism until it seemed that only a St. George could cut the knots. The Roosevelt-Truman Courts had slashed a gaping hole in the Constitution, and through that hole could now march all those who wanted to bring to Washington complete domination and control over every phase of our economic life—something never before possible under our Constitution. Thus we were carried a great distance along the totalitarian road. But the journey was by no means complete. Americans going about their business paid too little attention to what was happening to them. They still thought they were living in free, sovereign states that would protect them against the ultimate tyranny of an all-powerful central government.

In a way, they were right, for there remained two major bastions which the revolutionists had to take before their task was finished. One was the public schools, where the minds of future generations could be controlled. The job there was being done partially by the "modern" educationists—the progressivist revolutionaries —who, through "progressive" education, were under-educating class after class of young Americans in order to make them willing tools of the "new social order." But the outcries against them were rising. And the schools were still locally controlled. Hard as they had tried, the collectivists in Washington had so far been unable to bring the state and locally supported and managed public schools under their direction.

The other bastion was our awakening to the communist-socialist menace in our midst, and our efforts— through both state and national action—to protect ourselves, our institutions, and our liberties from the home-grown and imported practitioners of the worst tyranny the world had ever known.

We had a right to expect, with the first change of national administration in twenty years, that these two bastions at least would be protected. But it is one of the tragedies of our time that Eisenhower appointees to the Supreme Court, plus holdovers from the Roosevelt-Truman era, have given to those who would bring all power to the center the means to storm these last two bastions. We are thus brought face to face with perhaps the greatest constitutional crisis in our history.

# CHAPTER THIRTEEN

# Eisenhower's Chief Justice—Earl Warren

In September, 1953, following the death of Chief Justice Vinson, President Eisenhower appointed Earl Warren of California as the new Chief Justice. It was an amazing appointment in every way. For the first time in forty-three years, a man with no previous judicial experience was named directly to the post of Chief Justice of the United States. Warren's background was wholly political—Attorney-General of California and three times governor of the State. His smiling, happy personality and his ability seemingly to be all things to all men had won him the nomination of *both the Republican and Democratic parties*. This may seem no great feat in this day when, nationally, each party vies for the privilege of running better than the other our rapidly growing collectivist government. But at the time when Warren got both parties in his state to nominate him there was still, at least in the public mind and in the state organizations, a difference in principles between the two parties.

72

This did not deter the always cheerful Earl Warren from feeling equally comfortable in either camp.

So far as can be determined, Warren's appointment was the first occasion in our history when a president cited an appointee's political views as his reason for naming him to the chief justiceship. The President said Mr. Warren was a "middle-of-the-roader." That was before the term "modern Republicanism" was invented. They both mean the same thing, or, as one sapient observer recently remarked, an elephant trying to make a jackass of himself. It had been generally believed that the appointment would go to the late Arthur F. Vanderbilt of the New Jersey Supreme Court, a past president of the American Bar Association who had an impressive record as a jurist. But one day the then Attorney-General, Herbert Brownell, flew out to Sacramento, came back, and announced the Warren appointment. He probably could have saved himself the trip. Earl Warren had delivered the California vote to Eisenhower at the 1952 Republican Convention. Now he had his reward.

Frank Hanighen (*Human Events,* Jan. 6, 1958) has since reported that Warren had the President over a barrel. The deal at the convention was that if Warren could cast California's sixty-eight votes to seat the Eisenhower delegates from five states, instead of the regularly elected Taft delegations, Warren would get the first Supreme Court vacancy if Eisenhower became President. When Vinson died, it was Eisenhower's intention to move one of the associate justices up to Chief Justice and name Warren an associate justice. Brownell went to Sacramento so to inform Warren. But Governor Warren, despite his jollity, could be extremely cold and calculating where the interests of Earl Warren were concerned. He informed Brownell he had been promised the first vacancy on the Court; the first vacancy was the chief justiceship; that's what he wanted and that's what he intended to have. When Brownell returned to Washington and reported this to the President, Eisenhower gave in.

No one who followed closely Earl Warren's career should have been surprised at his subsequent actions as Chief Justice. The only surprising aspect of the appointment was that it came at the hands of a president whom the people had elected because they wanted a change in Washington. In the light of what we now know, the surprise has worn thin. But there is one group which never selects its pets without thorough familiarity with their views. This is the leftist organization known as Americans for Democratic Action, which is our modern-day equivalent of the old Socialist Party.

In late 1955, before it was known whether President Eisenhower would run for a second term, his Chief Justice was mentioned as a possible candidate. Joseph L. Rauh, president of the Americans for Democratic Action, declaring ADA would welcome Warren's candidacy, said: "It would be a great luxury for the American people to have a choice between Chief Justice Warren on the Republican ticket and such a man as Stevenson, Harriman, or Kefauver on the Democratic ticket. The American people couldn't lose either way." It certainly would be a "great luxury"—one they could ill afford: all they had to lose was their freedom. And it was reported that, while the labor bosses would prefer Stevenson,

Harriman, or Kefauver, in the event the GOP should carry the election they would find Warren a highly satisfactory candidate.

Governor Warren's views, which surely must have been known to the President when he named him to head the Court, were never such as to cause the "liberals" and leftists to love him less. He was quick to take up the cry of "McCarthyism." He didn't wait until '53 and '54, when this became a term of opprobrium among all the legions of the left. He adopted it earlier, just after the communists had invented the word to smother the efforts of the Senator from Wisconsin in exposing the left-wing elements in the American State Department. The cue was given by the national secretary of the Communist Party in May, 1950, when he issued this call to the forces of the left: *"I urge all Communist Party members, and all anti-Fascists to yield second place to none in the fight to rid the country of the fascist poison of McCarthyism."* (Of course, "fascists" in the Red lexicon were all those opposed to communism.) One month later, Earl Warren told a national governors' conference that he did not like "McCarthyism," that he thought it was hurting our prestige abroad and suggested it would be a very bad thing for the Republican Party to become saddled with it.

As Governor of California, Warren opposed loyalty oaths for teachers. He also tried to put over on the people of California—unsuccessfully—a compulsory health-insurance scheme. In plain English that means socialized medicine, one of the major planks in the platform of the socialist revolutionaries in America. At times, his parroting of leftist terminology became almost comical. When asked, in 1952, if he was in sympathy with legislative investigations of communist activities in California, he said, "I am in favor of the principle but not of the tactics that have been used at times." That was a favorite phrase of all the misguided "liberals" who shuddered at the thought of communists and their collaborators being treated otherwise than with kid gloves.

Warren, of course, went right down the line for foreign aid and complete submission of United States foreign policy to the vagaries of the United Nations. He said in 1952, "The United Nations should be the cornerstone of our foreign policy." And—shades of things to come— he was for a compulsory federal Fair Employment Practices Commission (FEPC), under which the federal bureaucrats could snoop into every big and little business in every state in the land and tell its proprietor whom he could and could not hire. He was also for ever more social security, government housing, government aid to farmers, and "world cooperation through the United Nations." He thus managed, while he was still in active political life, to be very highly thought of not only by the Republican standard bearer, but by Adlai Stevenson and Harry Truman as well. In fact, Truman once said of him that he was a Democrat and didn't know it.

As for congressional investigations of subversives, Warren said, in 1952: "The problem of ferreting out subversives is that of the FBI, acting directly under the President." Warren wanted to be President in 1952. Yet he had so little understanding of the function of the FBI that he did not seem to know that its major—and very important—function is gathering the facts and then presenting them to the proper government official for action. That's what it did, for instance, in the case of Harry Dexter White, Assistant Secretary of the Treasury, who was working for a communist espionage cell in Washington. The FBI gave the facts to President Truman, whereupon he gave White a big job in the International Monetary Fund. It took a congressional committee to place the facts before the American people.

Governor Warren also had his doubts about the Taft-Hartley Act. He thought it terribly unfair that union bosses should have to take an anticommunist oath when the heads of corporations weren't forced to do so too. But perhaps the best comment on Earl Warren's record, both before and after appointment, was supplied by the very left-wing magazine the *Nation*. It carried an article in July, 1956, in which it waxed lyrical over "the Warren Court." In fact, the article was subtitled "Turn to Liberalism," meaning, of course, the creeping socialism of the *Nation*. It even box-scored the justices, accordingly as they acted to suit the leftist philosophy of the *Nation* and its readers. And, lo and behold, Chief Justice Warren appeared with the high score of 73 percent, just below the scores of the *Nation's* heroes—Justices Black, Douglas, and Frankfurter.

It is not known whether Eisenhower was aware, when he named Warren to head the Court, of the precise functions of a chief justice. It was an awareness of those functions which led all our presidents in the past half century, save Eisenhower, to name chief justices with judicial experience. The chief justice's vote, of

course, is no greater or less than that of any other justice—he has just one vote. But his influence over the
Court can be great. First of all, the chief justice always
votes last on any decision before the Court. If there is a
close decision in which the members are divided evenly
—four to four—his will be the deciding vote. Also, if he is
on the majority side, it is he who will either write the decision himself or name the justice who will do so. And,
most important, the chief justice, as presiding officer of
the Court, is the first to put before his colleagues the issues involved in all cases that come before the Court.

Although President Eisenhower named Warren to the
chief justiceship of the Supreme Court in September,
1953, his appointment was not confirmed by the Senate
until the following March. A good many senators were
troubled by Warren's lack of experience for the job and
about his seeming agreement on many important issues
with the leftists and anti-anticommunists. But those
were the halcyon days of the "great change" in Washington, and the appointment went through by a voice
vote.

# CHAPTER FOURTEEN

# The *NAACP* versus *the 48 States*

Two months after the Senate confirmed the Chief Justice's appointment, on May 17, 1954, the Warren Supreme Court issued its revolutionary decision (Brown v. Board of Education)—a unanimous one—in the school-segregation cases.

What the Court did in that decision was not to settle the issue of segregation or integration of Negro and white pupils in the public schools. Racial issues are not settled by law—constitutional or otherwise. They are settled by time and the forbearance and patience of the people involved. One of the major human tragedies resulting from the Court's decision is that an issue that was well on its way to solution—slowly, to be sure, in some places—will now plague us for many years to come, intensified almost beyond reason by the Court's action.

But since ours is meant to be a government of law and not of men, the overwhelming tragedy for us all is that the Court, in its segregation decision, stormed one of those last remaining bastions of a free people we have previously mentioned—the locally controlled and supported public-school systems of the sovereign states. For, by that decision the Supreme Court handed to the central government a power it had never before possessed—the power to put its grasping and omnipotent hand into a purely local function. If the federal government can tell the public school in your town—whether in a northern, southern, western, or eastern state—who it shall or shall not admit, the next step is as logical as that winter follows fall. It will not be long before the socialist revolutionaries will have what they want—control by the central government of what to teach and what not to teach, how to teach it and how not to teach it in the public schools of America.

The legal defendants in the school cases were a few Southern states. But the real defendants were each and every one of the 48 sovereign states of the American Union and the Constitution they established for their own government.

The plaintiff who brought the cases before the Supreme Court is an organization known as the National Association for the Advancement of the Colored People (NAACP). It is a fairly old organization which started out with the avowed purpose of securing justice for Negroes who were discriminated against because of their race. But in the last decade or two, coincident with the rising wave of left-wing activity in America, it has become extremely militant.

The NAACP has always denied vehemently that it is communist or communist-dominated. They may be correct. But we do know that the delicate and dangerous field of race relations has always been, and still is, one of the favorite hunting grounds for the communist agitator to bring about the tensions, hatreds, and distortions so essential to his aims. And we have a right to wonder about an organization like the NAACP—which so vehemently disclaims any communist connections—when the records of the House Committee on Un-American Activities over the past 15 years reveal communist, communist-front, fellow-traveling, or subversive organizations or activities on the part of the president, chairman of the board, honorary chairman, 11 of 28 vice-presidents, 28 of 47 directors, and a number of other officials. In February, 1958, Dr. J. B. Matthews, a leading authority on communist fronts, testifying before a state legislative committee, declared: "Public records show that 145 of the 236 persons, or 61 percent, listed as national officers of the NAACP have records of affiliation with communist organizations."

The NAACP was started in New York City by five founders. One was a social worker and descendant of an old-time abolitionist—Miss Mary Ovington White. Another was a communist writer named William E. Walling. The third and fourth were Dr. Henry Moskowitz and Oswald Garrison Villard (the grandson of William Lloyd Garrison). The fifth—and only Negro founder—was W.E.B. DuBois, who remained, through the years, NAACP's leading light. He had a communist-front record covering eight single-spaced typewritten pages. In 1957, President Eisenhower saw fit to send greetings to the NAACP, but his State Department was unable to issue a passport to DuBois because of his unsavory record.

This, then, was the plaintiff in the school-segregation cases. The defendants, as we have said, were the 48 sovereign states, each with its own locally controlled public-school system. The Supreme Court of the United States, under Chief Justice Warren, decided the cases in favor of the NAACP and told the 48 sovereign American states, in effect, that the federal government in Washington henceforth would set the standards of admission to their state schools.

# CHAPTER FIFTEEN

# The Supreme Court Makes a Law

In order to bring about this revolution of totalitarian proportions, it was necessary for Chief Justice Warren and his colleagues to ignore 165 years of Supreme Court history and a decision of the Court that had stood unchallenged for nearly 60 years.

In 1896 a case (Plessy v. Ferguson) came before the Court involving a state law. Louisiana had a statute providing for segregation of races on railroad trains. The law was challenged on the ground that it violated the 14th Amendment to the Constitution. The Supreme Court decided that, since the Louisiana law provided for "separate but equal" facilities, it was not in violation of the Constitution. In other words, the Court affirmed that when a state provided the same facilities, even though they be physically separated, for whites and Negroes (or impliedly for girls and boys or men and women) it was fulfilling its duty under the Constitution. In this case the Court was carrying out its historic function under the Constitution. The problem of segregating or not segregating the races was a state problem. The State of Louisiana, exercising its sovereign function, passed a law providing for segregation. The only question to be settled by the Court was whether or not that law violated any provision of the Constitution. The Court did not say to Louisiana: you must segregate, or you must not segregate. It simply said that because the Louisiana law, while providing for segregation, also provided for separate but equal facilities, Louisiana had fulfilled her obligation under the 14th Amendment to the Constitution.

Actually, this was not the first, or the last, time the question came before the Court. It arose at least six separate times in a period of 75 years. And each time the Supreme Court upheld the doctrine of equal but separate facilities.

Forty-six years ago, in 1912, Justice Charles Evans Hughes, speaking for the Court, remarked that the question could "no longer be considered an open one." In other words, under the Constitution it was settled. This naturally raises the query: why did the Supreme Court agree to hear the school cases in the first place? The Court is its own judge of what cases it shall and shall not consider and decide upon. (This brings us up against a situation in the Court which has been too little publicized— that of the role of those "bright young men" who serve as law clerks to the justices. We will consider them, and their influence, more fully a little later).

Following the 1896 decision, the Supreme Court in several cases *involving schools** upheld that eminently

---

* See especially Cummings v. Board of Education, 175 U.S. 528 (1899) and Gong Lum v. Rice, 275 U.S. 78 (1927).

fair—and constitutional—interpretation of the 14th Amendment and the rights of the states. We must remember that only the states—three-fourths of them—can ratify an amendment to the Constitution. The highest courts of 23 of the states which adopted the amendment had held that it did not abolish segregation. Of equal importance is the fact—so well stated by James Jackson Kilpatrick (in *The Sovereign States*) after a thorough review of all the evidence—that: *"Neither the Congress that proposed the 14th Amendment, nor a single one of the thirty-seven States that considered it, understood that the amendment, of and by itself, outlawed segregation by race in the public schools."* There can be no better evidence of the truth of this statement than that the Congress which approved the 14th Amendment *simultaneously passed a law establishing segregated schools in the District of Columbia.* And when the Supreme Court included such a distinguished judge as Chief Justice Taft, and such heroes of the "liberals" as Justices Holmes, Brandeis, and Stone, it said unanimously that segregation in public schools had been "many times decided to be within the constitutional power of the State legislature to settle *without interference of the federal courts under the Federal Constitution"* (italics added).

Faced with a body of law and precedent like this, what was the Warren Supreme Court to do? It did something unprecedented in our history. It threw out the window the Constitution and all previous Court interpretations, and arrogated to itself a function reserved only for our representatives in Congress. *It wrote a new law—something the Supreme Court has no right to do—*and proclaimed it the law of the land by judicial fiat. The Congress of the United States—the only body to which the Constitution gives law-making powers—*has never passed a law forcing the races to be mixed in the public schools*. If it had, it would then have been up to the Supreme Court to say whether the law was constitutional or not. In the light of our past constitutional and judicial history, a lawful Court would have had to declare such a law unconstitutional, since it would be an obvious invasion by the Congress of a purely state function.

But the Warren Court did what Justice Black (who concurred) had once accused President Truman of doing —it usurped the legislative function of the Congress. It wrote a law—a law based on the very doubtful psycho-sociological precept that if the races went to separate schools, it would retard the development of the Negro children. It might just as well have said that the development of the girls who attend Julia Richman High School in New York City is being retarded because there are no boys in the school! Dr. Pitirim A. Sorokin, one of our most distinguished students of sociology, has said of this combination of sociology and psychology that both "are in a blind alley of subjective and evanescent hearsay trivia. In our courts most of this 'hearsay stuff' is rejected as evidence." But not in the Supreme Court of the United States. It wrote a law based on this pseudo-science of "hearsay trivia." It departed entirely from the constitutional question involved, and took upon itself the issuance of a ukase in the field of pedagogy—and a doubtful pedagogy at that, since it is based on a doubtful psycho-sociological "science." It said that Negro children would be retarded in their development if they were not mixed with white children in the schools because this "generates a feeling of inferiority as to their status." Those are the Court's words.

This brought a stinging rejoinder (in the Richmond *Times-Dispatch*, Aug. 23, 1955) from Mrs. Zora Neale Hurston, a most distinguished American writer and playwright, who is a Negro. She is one of the few members of her race who have had the courage to speak out despite the pressures of the NAACP. Mrs. Hurston declared:

The whole matter revolves around the self respect of my people. How much satisfaction can I get from a Court order for somebody to associate with me who does not wish me near them? The American Indian has never been spoken of as a minority and chiefly because there is no whine in the Indian. Certainly he fought, and valiantly, for his lands—and rightfully so. But it is inconceivable of an Indian to seek forcible association with anyone. His well-known pride and self-respect would save him from that. I take the Indian position. . . .

I regard the ruling of the United States Supreme Court as insulting rather than honoring my race . . . In the ruling on segregation, the unsuspecting nation might have witnessed a trial balloon. A relatively safe one, since it is sectional and on a matter not likely to arouse other sections of the nation to the support of the South. If it goes off fairly well, a precedent has been established. Government by fiat can replace the Constitution.

Yet it was to enforce this unlawful "law" of the Supreme Court that we have since had the sorry spectacle of the President of the United States sending federal troops into a sovereign American state.

The principle involved in the President's action in Little Rock, Arkansas, had nothing to do with the merits of integration or segregation. Sending federal troops into a sovereign American state under such circumstances was a clearly illegal act by the President. The United States Code—the body of law which governs the United States—contains a section passed in 1878 known as the "*posse comitatus* act." It was restated and recodified by Congress on August 10, 1956. It states:

Whoever, except in cases and circumstances expressly authorized by the Constitution or act of Congress, willfully uses any part of the Army or the Air Force as a *posse comitatus* or otherwise to execute the laws shall be fined not more than $10,000 or imprisoned not more than two years, or both.

Only a nation drugged by twenty years of communist-socialist propaganda, and a group of politicians in Congress with one eye on the Negro vote in the North, could have sat by and permitted the Executive to get away with this unlawful intrusion upon the rights of the sovereign states. We have since had an interesting, though inadvertent, admission of the illegality not only of the President's action but of the Supreme Court's as well, from the New York *Times* (Dec. 8, 1957).

When the federal government forced the Governor of

Arkansas to withdraw the state militia from a high school in Little Rock, some rioting broke out around the school before the federal troops arrived. The federal government made threats about the arrests and prosecutions which awaited the rioters when the federal law-enforcement officers caught up with them. Several months went by and nothing happened, so the New York *Times* sent a reporter to find out why. He declared that the Department of Justice was not to blame for failing to prosecute, because—in the words of the New York *Times:* "The basic fact is that, under the Constitution, the job of maintaining order locally is given almost entirely to the states, not to the federal government. Thus the federal government has no constitutional power to punish an ordinary breach of the peace or assault." But the gravamen of the *Times'* story was this: "It [the federal government] can reach that kind of offense only if some federal right is involved, *and then only if Congress has passed a specific statute to cover the offense"* (italics added).

But so far as the Supreme Court's decision in the segregation cases is concerned, the socialist revolutionaries in America now have what they want—the opening wedge for complete control of education by the central government.

# CHAPTER SIXTEEN

# The Court's "Authorities"

What possible excuse could the justices give for this unwarranted seizure of power? Unless one of the justices some day sees fit to reveal the story, no one will ever know what went on inside the Court while the school cases were pending. These cases first came before the Court in 1952 and were scheduled and rescheduled for hearings several times before a decision was finally rendered in 1954. It was Chief Justice Warren who delivered—and presumably wrote—that revolutionary decision. And it is Warren who is credited with "harmonizing" the Court and bringing about the unanimous decree. Warren, who likes to be liked by everybody, is the "hail-fellow-well-met" type. He calls all the other justices by their first names, and enjoys flouting precedent to such an extent that he appeared on the platform at a meeting of the American Bar Association in London—gathered to hear an address from the Prime Minister—in a bright chocolate-colored suit with a gray tie. All the other distinguished guests on the platform wore formal dress, morning clothes, or dark suits. One American lady present at the meeting thought Mr. Warren should have remembered that he was Chief Justice of the United States and said, "If he didn't know any better, somebody should have told him."

Despite the Chief Justice's good fellowship, however, his legal knowledge was admittedly rusty. One admirer said he "studied far into the night to polish up his knowledge of constitutional law." More objective observers believe it was Felix Frankfurter who supplied the "studies" and cajoled the more reluctant members of the Court into going along with the decision. Justice Frankfurter, together with Justice Douglas, were two of the early swallowers of that "sociological jurisprudence" which Professor Sorokin has so aptly called "hearsay trivia."

In any case, the "authorities" to which the Chief Justice and his colleagues turned to justify their unlawful decision are almost beyond belief. One of them was a so-called "social science expert," named K. B. Clark, employed by the NAACP—*the principal plaintiff that brought the cases before the Court*. It was a very strange procedure, to say the least, for the Court to cite as an "authority" an employee of one of the litigants—and to do so *after* the hearings were over, so that the defendants had no chance to reply to or refute the arguments of such an "authority."

Another "authority" to whom the Court turned to justify its decision was a leading exponent of progressive or "modern" education—Theodore Brameld. In fact, he was one of those in the forefront of the drive which

has so successfully undereducated several generations
of American children in order to make them into the
compliantly ignorant mass of the "new social order" of
socialism in America. Besides this, he has been cited by
various government agencies as having been connected
*with at least 10 communist-front organizations.* The
justices could hardly have been in ignorance of his record,
since some of the citations were made by the Attorney-
General's office when it was in charge of Justice Tom
Clark, and by an official publication of the State of
California when Chief Justice Warren was governor.

Still another "authority" of the Court was E. Franklin
Frazier, a sociologist who had *18 communist-front con-
nections to his credit.* He was the author of a book on the
Negro—full of that psycho-sociological "hearsay trivia"
—which the Warren Court cited in its decision. The
Court thus joined hands with the Communist *Daily
Worker* and Communist *Daily People's World* which
gave the book their blessing. So did the Communist
Workers Book Shop Catalog, which advertises only
books acceptable to the Communist Party.

First and foremost among the Court's "authorities,"
however, was a book compiled and partly written by Gun-
nar Myrdal, a Swedish socialist. He had no knowledge
whatever of race relations in America. He was brought
over here and given a grant by the Carnegie Foundation
to produce a book on the subject. As he is a socialist, his
contempt for the American Constitution is complete. He
called it "impractical and unsuited to modern conditions"
and said its adoption was "nearly a plot against the
common people." This Swedish socialist had sixteen col-

laborators who contributed 272 articles and portions of his book. *Every one of these 16 had communist-front affiliations.* One of them, for instance, was that same W.E.B. DuBois, of the NAACP, who could not get a passport from the State Department because of his record. But he, his fifteen communist-front collaborators, and their socialist editor passed muster with the Supreme Court of the United States. The Swedish socialist subsequently wound up in the United Nations, but even that body of outright and hooded leftists couldn't stomach his acceptance of communist statistics and in 1957 he had to resign.

When the Court overturned all previous decisions in the school cases, it said, speaking through Chief Justice Warren: "Whatever may have been the extent of psychological knowledge at the time of Plessy v. Ferguson, this finding is amply supported by modern authority." These, then, were the "modern authorities" used by the Supreme Court to overturn 165 years of American constitutional law.

The Court, of course, had to clothe its use of these "authorities" in some constitutional raiment, no matter how synthetic. It could not just say that a group of pro-communist writers has figured out that the Negro will "feel inferior" if he goes to separate but equal schools, and so we hereby declare that the races must be mixed in the schools. It therefore hit upon a phrase in the 14th Amendment to the Constitution which reads: ". . . nor shall any State . . . deny to any person within its jurisdiction the equal protection of the laws."

The Court's action has led many serious students of

our constitutional history to question once again the validity of the 14th Amendment itself. There can be no doubt that the Amendment was "adopted" under odd circumstances in one of the most shameful periods of our national life. After the War between the States—the Civil War—the Southern states adopted the 13th Amendment to the Constitution. That is the amendment which abolished slavery. The federal government accepted this ratification by the Southern states of the 13th Amendment and it became part of the Constitution. But when the 14th Amendment came before the legislatures of the Southern states, they turned it down. But in this case the federal government did not accept their action. We were in the throes of the shameful "Reconstruction Era" in the South. Not only were all Southern members of the House and Senate deprived of their seats, but the federal government ordered troops to take charge of the legislatures of the Southern states. "Reconstruction" or puppet legislatures were set up, and it was these—under duress of federal troops—which ratified the 14th Amendment.

That was nearly ninety years ago, and no Supreme Court since that time has ever ruled on whether or not such a "ratification" of the 14th Amendment was legal. But it would seem that those who raise the question once again—no matter how sound their reasoning may be—would appear to be rather in the position of beating a dead horse. A whole body of law has become imbedded in our system based on the amendment during the long years since its passage. Any value that might flow from invalidation of the amendment would be very much overshadowed by the chaos that would result from the abrogation of those laws founded on another phrase, that no state shall "deprive any person of life, liberty, or property, without due process of law."

In any case, those who would oppose the Warren Supreme Court's unlawful seizure of power have a complete answer even assuming the validity of the 14th Amendment. As we have pointed out, innumerable earlier Supreme Courts, as well as the highest courts of 23 of the sovereign states which adopted the amendment, have declared that "equal protection of the laws" is fulfilled in the provision of separate but equal facilities; plus the fact that the Congress and the 37 states which adopted the amendment were clear that it did not apply to the public schools. And the final section of the 14th Amendment itself puts the Warren Court thoroughly beyond the pale of legal and constitutional action in its school decision. That section reads: "The Congress shall have the power to enforce, by appropriate legislation, the provisions of this article."

Congress has never passed "appropriate legislation" declaring that the races must be mixed in the public schools. On the contrary, it passed legislation providing for segregated schools in the only educational system over which it has jurisdiction—that of the District of Columbia. The Supreme Court simply usurped the legislative power from Congress, and, on the "authority" of a handful of leftist pseudo-scientists, is ruling the operation of our local schools by judicial fiat.

# CHAPTER SEVENTEEN

# More "Packees"—Jackson, Burton, Clark, and Minton

But who were the justices who concurred in such infamy? We have already had a look at five of them—Chief Justice Warren and Justices Frankfurter, Reed, Black, and Douglas. The other four justices on the bench at the time of the segregation decision were Jackson, Burton, Clark, and Minton.

Robert H. Jackson was another of the Roosevelt appointees to the Court—and another with no previous judicial experience. In fact, he didn't even have a law degree. He was born in Spring Creek, Pa., in 1892, and spent one year in a "quickie" law school in Albany, N.Y., but skipped the other year required for a sheepskin. However, he was later admitted to the bar and was a practicing lawyer in upstate New York when he was brought to Washington in 1934 as general counsel of the Internal Revenue Bureau. While there, he handed down a ruling allowing the busy money-making wife of President Roosevelt to deduct more than the maximum 15 percent of earnings for charitable contributions. The more one can claim for charitable contributions, the lower the tax rate on overall income and thus the more the taxpayer can keep for himself.

After that, his rise was rapid. He became an Assistant Attorney-General, then Solicitor-General, then Attorney-General—where he led the fight for Roosevelt's court-packing scheme before Congress. In 1941 he was named to the High Court.

Justice Jackson had a caustic tongue and a quick temper. While he was on the Court, he carried on a bitter feud with Justice Black which perhaps cost Jackson the chief justiceship and finally had the "liberal" Supreme Court washing its dirty linen in public. At this late day, it is almost impossible to separate the facts from the rumors about this feud, but essentially here is what happened.

Justice Jackson evidently had some sort of promise from Roosevelt—a promise that was renewed by President Truman—that when Chief Justice Stone retired or died, Jackson would be named Chief Justice. Stone died after Truman became President, and there seems to be little doubt that Truman had every intention of making Jackson Chief Justice. However, in the meantime, a case had come before the Court which resulted in a five-to-four decision. The majority decided in favor of the side which was represented by a former law partner of Justice Black. Jackson wrote a stinging dissent in the case. In the privacy of the court chambers, court attachés could overhear angry and immoderate words between the two justices. Jackson thought Black should have disqualified himself, since a former law partner of his was involved in the case, while Black considered the implication that he would decide a case on such a basis an insult to his judicial honor. There was no rule of the Court covering such circumstances.

Then Jackson went off to Germany to preside over the Nuremberg trials. While he was there, Truman named Fred Vinson Chief Justice, mainly, as we have noted, to see if he couldn't quiet the name-calling and personal bickering on the Court which was threatening to break out in public. At about the same time, the loser in the case over which Justices Black and Jackson exchanged angry words applied for a rehearing on the ground that Black ought to have disqualified himself. Jackson, brooding in Nuremberg about the fact that he had been passed over for the chief justiceship, and with the concurrence of Justice Frankfurter, issued a public blast against Justice Black—and the feud was out in the open on the front pages of all the newspapers. Jackson declared in Nuremberg that he had made the whole thing public because Black had threatened that if he did so it would "mean a declaration of war." Justice Black held his peace and made no reply. Eventually the furor died down.

That's the way the story appeared to the public. But behind the scenes appeared the hand of the inveterate meddler, Justice Frankfurter. Washington gossip—which, surprisingly enough, often turns out to have a grain of truth in it—had it that the real reason Truman didn't appoint Jackson to head the Court was that former Chief Justice Hughes and Justice Roberts had gone to the President and told him they didn't feel Jackson had the proper temperament to be Chief Justice—he was too quick-tempered and tactless. Robert S. Allen, the Washington correspondent, later reported that Justice Frankfurter, who was always writing letters, wrote one to Justice Jackson in Nuremberg in which he made a statement which Allen said was completely untrue—that Black had gone to Truman and told him he would not serve on the Court under Jackson. In Nuremberg, Jackson, of course, had no way of knowing that the trouble-making Frankfurter had concocted the story out of whole cloth. He thereupon released his public blast against Black and brought the Supreme Court down to the level of gutter politics. That, at least, is the story according to Washington news gatherers.

A recent laudatory biography of Justice Jackson (*America's Advocate: Robert H. Jackson* by Eugene C. Gerhardt) attempts to justify Jackson's open blast at Black strictly on the grounds of Jackson's belief in the legal proprieties. The author says Jackson was angry with Black because Black cast the deciding vote in the case in which his former law partner was involved and tried to pressure his colleagues into keeping quiet about it, and that the purpose behind the whole thing (having to do with a portal-to-portal pay case) was to enable John L. Lewis to win a strike. Yet the fact remains that Jackson thought he was going to be made Chief Justice, that he wasn't, and that, if Allen's story is correct, Frankfurter told him it was Black's doing which blocked his appointment.

It is impossible, as we have said, to separate the gossip from the facts. Yet the act with which Frankfurter is supposed to have charged Black—going to Truman to stop Jackson's appointment—does seem out of character. Justice Black, whatever his "liberal" views, was reserved and quiet, keeping very much to himself. He had had enough trouble when he first went on the Court, what with the Klan charges and the fact that the Chief Justice (Hughes at the time) had gotten Black's negative vote when Black was in the Senate and Hughes was up for confirmation. Black had behaved himself admirably in his personal relations on the Court in a trying situation and had eventually won the respect of his colleagues, particularly as he was hardworking and industrious and never shirked his share of the duties—as Frankfurter was wont to do. Frankfurter was so busy with his string-pulling that he seldom had time to attend to the Court's routine business.

As for Justice Jackson, he evidently reached some sort of rapprochement with his colleagues when he returned from Nuremberg, for he remained among them—a somewhat embittered man. He had seen the chief justiceship of the United States slip from his grasp. The Nuremberg trials had not added to his reputation. He could not help being aware of the fact that many respected men in his own profession were shocked at a justice of the Supreme Court of the United States sitting as both judge and prosecutor in a series of trials in which he was establishing and administering *ex post facto* law. Much as Americans hated the Nazi war lords, it was completely alien to the American tradition of law to prosecute men for criminal acts which were not declared to be so until long after the fact. As the late Senator Robert A. Taft had the courage to point out, the Nuremberg trials over which Justice Jackson presided will forever remain a blot on the escutcheon of American jurisprudence.

As the years went on, Jackson—originally an ardent New Dealer—became somewhat more conservative in his views, but in the segregation decision he harked back to his former feeling about the Constitution. He said in 1940: "The national government has won its long fight to free itself of unwarranted limitations." And he once exulted that the Supreme Court "had established a supremacy that could deny important powers to both state and nation on principles nowhere found in the Constitution itself." Jackson died five months after the segregation decision, leaving the Court open to another Eisenhower appointment to which we will come in a moment.

Justice Harold H. Burton was a Truman appointee—somewhat the same brand of "modern Republican" as Chief Justice Warren. He was a crony of President Truman's from his Senate days. He was born in 1888 in Jamaica Plain, Mass., went to Bowdoin College and later to Harvard Law, where he got his law degree in 1912. He then settled in Cleveland, Ohio, to practice law. His claim to competence for the Supreme Court appointment was that he had once been mayor of Cleveland. He had no judicial experience whatever and became known as the member of the bench who wrote the fewest opinions. But Washington party going was something else again—it was a rare party indeed that was not graced by the presence of Justice Burton. He is still on the Court at this writing, and in the last year or two has joined in several dissents in cases involving communists, against the overwhelming rush of the left-wing majority.

Justice Tom C. Clark of Texas became, in the 1956-1957 session of the Court, the chief and often the lone dissenter. He is a native Texan, having been born in Dallas in 1899. He got his college education and his law degree from the University of Texas. But Justice Clark went along in the segregation decision and, in fact, was the author of one of the worst subsequent decisions (Slochower v. Bd. of Higher Education) of the Court—that which takes away from a state or city the right to fire a teacher who refuses to reveal his communist connections.

Clark was a Truman appointee, also with no judicial experience. Most of his career he spent in New Deal and Fair Deal bureaus, winding up as Truman's Attorney-General. It has been said that Truman named him to the Court to put him beyond the reach of congressional investigators who were looking into the mess of corruption and "fixing" during those days. However, a House Judiciary Committee later absolved him of any personal wrong-doing, but reprimanded him for "withholding his cooperation" from the committee's work.

Justice Sherman Minton, the last of the nine who rendered the segregation decision, was the only one who had had any real previous judicial experience. But it is interesting to note how he got it. He was born in Georgetown, Indiana, in 1890, got his law degree from Indiana University in 1915, and began practicing law in New Albany in his native state. In 1934 he was elected to the Senate from Indiana. He was an ardent New Dealer who fought hard to put over Roosevelt's court-packing plan. He was noted for his willingness to do anything Roosevelt wanted—in fact, he himself boasted that he was a "rubber stamp" and a "100 percent New Dealer." After six years of this, the voters of Indiana got fed up and defeated him.

Minton was wandering around Washington looking for a job when Roosevelt named him to a $10,000-a-year post as a White House administrative assistant. Four months later a circuit judge in Chicago died, leaving vacant a $17,000 job, and Roosevelt handed it to Minton. There he remained for eight years, until Truman plucked him from the Chicago bench in 1949 and put him on the Supreme Court.

In a recent term of the Court, Justice Minton joined Justices Reed and Clark in several dissents against the ever-increasing assaults on the Constitution by the majority of the Court. But at the end of the Court's work in 1956 he resigned and gave to President Eisenhower his third appointment to the Court. Justice Stanley Reed's subsequent resignation in 1957 gave the President his fourth appointment.

These were the men—Warren, Minton, Clark, Burton, Jackson, Douglas, Frankfurter, Reed, and Black—who, on the "authority" of a batch of left-wing nobodies, did what no Congress of the United States had ever permitted. They put the hand of the central government directly into the public school systems of the American states.

# CHAPTER EIGHTEEN

# Ike Goes on Packing—Harlan, Brennan, and Whittaker

It is this Court as constituted at the time of the school decision, and as partly reconstituted by President Eisenhower with the appointments of Justices Harlan, Brennan, and Whittaker, in addition to Chief Justice Warren, which stormed that final bastion mentioned earlier—our efforts to protect ourselves against the communist conspiracy in America.

Justice Charles E. Whittaker, who replaced Justice Reed, we may dismiss quickly since he was too recent an appointee to have had any part in this foray. He was born (in 1901) and brought up on a Kansas farm and worked his way through the law school of the University of Kansas City, where he later had a successful law practice. He has been a lifelong Republican and is considered by lawyers a "middle-of-the-roader." He himself refuses to say whether he is a "modern" Republican or not. Justice Whittaker had some judicial experience of rather brief duration—eight months on the United States Circuit

Court of Appeals and District Judge for two years before that—both appointments at the hands of President Eisenhower.

Justice John Marshall Harlan, appointed in 1955 to replace Justice Jackson, was also rather short on judicial experience. He served one year on the Circuit Court of Appeals in New York. It is believed he was appointed to that post because Eisenhower contemplated eventually giving him a Supreme Court appointment, and was sensitive to criticism of the Court because of its lack of judicial experience. He was born in Chicago in 1899, but later became a New Yorker. He is a graduate of Princeton and also a Rhodes Scholar. He got his law degree from New York Law School in 1924 and in 1932 became a partner in one of the largest law firms in New York.

Justice Harlan seemed to possess a naïveté unbecoming a Justice of the Supreme Court. He had been a member of the Atlantic Union Committee since 1952. During the hearings on his appointment, he was asked about this. His answer revealed that he was either a very naïve man or that he took the senators for fools. He said the Atlantic Union Committee was only an instrumentality "trying to bring about collective action in defense against communism." Senator William E. Jenner then read to Mr. Harlan the purposes of the Atlantic Union Committee—a common defense, a common currency, common trade, and *a common citizenship* among the United States and the Western European nations. Harlan expressed great astonishment that he had been supporting a group which favors the sinking of American sovereignty into a union with Great Britain and other European countries.

There had never been any secret about the Atlantic Union's purposes. It spends a good deal of money publicizing them and working to get congressmen and senators to pass a resolution calling an international convention to put them into effect. Justice Harlan spent four years on the advisory council of the Atlantic Union Committee. But only when the senators confronted him with the facts about its purposes did he disassociate himself from its objectives.

In fact, Justice Harlan's naïveté seemed to know no bounds. A question of vital importance which has been before the American people in recent years is whether or not a treaty—made by the President with only the consent of the Senate—can override the Constitution. There are those amongst our internationally minded one-worlders who insist that it can. Unfortunately, the Constitution itself is somewhat vague on the point—no doubt because the framers who fought for American independence did not conceive of a time when it would be willingly relinquished by such a subterfuge. Even John Foster Dulles, in an unguarded moment before he became President Eisenhower's Secretary of State, declared that a treaty could conceivably destroy the Constitution and even the Bill of Rights. To correct this flaw in the Constitution, Senator John Bricker of Ohio had had before the people since 1951 an amendment to the Constitution—known as the Bricker Amendment. At one session of the Senate it came within one vote of the required two thirds for passage.

Justice Harlan, in 1955, was asked about his views on the Bricker Amendment. His reply was that he had been too busy with his law practice to know what it was all about. It had not only been before the country for nearly five years, but had been overwhelmingly ratified by the American Bar Association's House of Delegates three times. Justice Harlan was a member of the American Bar Association.

In the light of Justice Harlan's seeming ignorance on these points, it is interesting to note that one of his most ardent boosters was Judge Joseph Proskauer of New York. In fact, they formed a mutual admiration society, Justice Harlan also praising Judge Proskauer highly. In 1948 Judge Proskauer, together with Dr. Philip Jessup (of the communist-infiltrated Institute of Pacific Relations) and *Alger Hiss* filed a brief before the Supreme Court of the United States as "friends of the court" (*amici curiae*). The case involved a restrictive covenant and it was the contention of Proskauer, Jessup, and Hiss that the covenant was illegal *because it violated the United Nations Charter*. The United Nations Charter controlled domestic law in the United States!

One other interesting sidelight on Justice Harlan, which of course may not be significant, is that his grandfather was the lone dissenter in the Plessy v. Ferguson case of 1896, which affirmed the principle of separate but equal facilities.

Justice William J. Brennan, Jr., of New Jersey, who succeeded Justice Minton, had at least had considerable judicial experience as a judge of New Jersey's Supreme Court. He is a native of New Jersey, having been born in

Newark in 1906. He attended the University of Pennsylvania and got his law degree from Harvard Law School
in 1931. One of his teachers at Harvard Law was Professor—now Justice—Felix Frankfurter. Nobody seemed
to know much about Brennan's views when he was appointed, though one official described him as a "middle-of-the-roader" (another one!)—this time a "modern
Democrat." It is believed he was appointed chiefly because he was a Catholic and there had been no Catholic
on the Court since Murphy's death. But if the President
was looking for a man of real Supreme Court caliber
whose only other qualification was his religion, he had
two of them right under his nose in Washington. One
had been Chief Justice of the United States Court of Appeals there since 1935—Judge Harold M. Stephens. Another—with the additional qualification of being a member of the President's own party—was a circuit judge of
the same court—John A. Danaher. Both were Catholics.
But here was the rub. Judge Stephens was known as a
strict constitutionalist and Judge Danaher as a conservative.

There seems little doubt that it was the "liberal"-
internationalist crowd of "modern" Republicans around
New York and New Jersey who sold Justice Brennan to
the President. He wasn't on the Court very long before he
gave us a good peek into his mind. In his very first opinion,
he wrote the decision (Jencks v. U.S.) opening the FBI
files to the communists, to say nothing of assorted crooks,
grafters, and narcotics peddlers. Fortunately, Congress
corrected this outrageous decision somewhat before it ad-
journed in the summer of 1957. And, to his credit, Justice

Clark wrote a stinging dissent to Justice Brennan's decision. But Justices Warren, Black, Frankfurter, Harlan, Douglas, and Burton went along with Justice Brennan.

Justice Brennan saw the fruit of his decision on December 31, 1957, when the government asked a U.S. District Judge to dismiss its case against Clinton E. Jencks. Jencks was a labor-union official convicted of filing a false non-communist affidavit. When he appealed to the Supreme Court, Justice Brennan, for the Court, ordered a new trial for Jencks, on the ground that his FBI dossier was not made available to him. District Judge R. E. Thomason reluctantly granted the government's request to drop the case against Jencks. But he could not resist pointing out (for Justice Brennan's benefit, perhaps?) that Jencks was tried by a fair and impartial jury and found guilty. Judge Thomason added: "This court thought he was guilty then and thinks he is guilty now."

Even more serious is the fact that in January, 1958, the U. S. Court of Appeals in Washington reversed the finding of the government's Subversive Activities Control Board that the Communist Party of the United States must register as a subversive organization. Why? Because under Justice Brennan's ruling in the Jencks case, the *Communist Party had not been shown the secret FBI reports on its activities.*

Justice Brennan, in his brief tenure on the Court, has won himself a place in the hearts of our "liberals" and leftists. He has voted almost without a break with Black, Douglas, and Warren.

# CHAPTER NINETEEN

# Behind the Black Robes

Before we go into the shocking aid which the justices of the Supreme Court have rendered to the communist conspiracy in America, it might be well to take a look behind those black robes at what are known as the "bright young men."

When we visit the chamber of the Supreme Court of the United States, we see sitting before us, high above the audience and the disputing attorneys, nine imposing, black-robed justices. But behind the justices, in the inner reaches of the beautiful Supreme Court building, sit eighteen young men through whose hands pass much of the work of the Court. They serve the justices for only a year or two and then are replaced by others of their kind. During their service to the Court, we seldom see them or hear of them. But some of them have gone on to fame of a kind. Dean Acheson was one of them, and so was Alger Hiss. Another, who served Justice Frankfurter, later served a term in jail in a vote-fraud case in his native state.

Many others, of course, have attained respected and useful places in the legal profession and in politics.

These bright young men are the law clerks of the justices of the Supreme Court. As of the 1957 session of the Court, seven justices had two clerks each, Justice Douglas had one, and Chief Justice Warren had three—eighteen in all. They are picked by the individual justices for whom they will work, and are taken from among the top performers of the graduates of leading law schools, generally on the recommendation of the deans.

Quite naturally, this brings up the question of how much influence these young men exercise on the justices and what part they have played in the type of decisions we have been getting from the Court these past two decades. First of all, it is beyond belief that a justice would choose as his law clerk a young man diametrically opposed to the justice's views. Second, these young men are the products of schools and universities which have been thoroughly infiltrated—in some cases saturated—with left-wing thinking. Six of the eighteen, for instance, serving the justices in 1957 came from the Law School of Harvard and three others from Yale. Yale, and particularly Harvard, have been hot-beds of New Deal-collectivist-left-wing teaching in recent years.

Washington, D.C., is, of course, the breeding ground of the genus known as ghost writers—those who pen the words that appear over another's name. Their habitat is sometimes the halls of Congress, but more often the government bureaus, the Cabinet, and the White House. And many believe that the ghostly art is practiced also in the inner sanctums of at least some of our Supreme Court justices, by these bright young law clerks. There are Supreme Court justices, of course, who have been perfectly capable of writing their own opinions. But there are also those who cannot—which is still another commentary on the type of Supreme Court appointments we have had at the hands of our last three presidents. And if a judge is inclined to indolence, or is not very sure of his own legal capabilities, or is busily engaged in activities outside the Court, he is liable to lean very heavily on his law clerks when the time comes to write an opinion.

However, some scraps of evidence have begun to appear, so that we need not speculate on this score. Justice Minton, for example, after his retirement from the Court, was asked if his clerks helped in drafting opinions. He replied: "In my case, after an opinion was written I submitted it to the boys for their comments and criticisms. And if *their criticisms were valid the opinion was rewritten*" (italics added). It is important to remember that "the boys" have just graduated from law school, that they have never practiced law, and that some of them are not yet even members of the bar.

Even more impressive evidence is supplied in a biography of Chief Justice Stone by Alpheus Thomas Mason (Viking Press). The Chief Justice is quoted as saying at one time: "I am a good deal troubled by the dissenting opinion which Justice Black has just circulated . . . He states a good deal which counsel did not take the trouble to present . . . I see in Justice Black's dissent the handiwork of someone other than the nominal author." And the same book points out that two paragraphs in a historic footnote to one of Justice Stone's own opinions were written by his law clerk. The clerk, Louis Lusky, said Stone "adopted it almost as drafted, simply toning down a couple of overemphatic words."

But it is in the *selection* of cases that will come before the Court for review and decision that these bright young men come into their own. Each year anywhere from 1,500 to 2,000 appeals are made to the Supreme Court to hear and decide cases which have been settled one way or another in the lower courts. Obviously, a great number of them are outside the jurisdiction of the Court. Or they may involve precedents in the law so well established that a review by the High Court, assuming the lower court has followed those precedents, would be a waste of time. Or they may be cases similar to or identical with ones previously passed upon by the Supreme Court and therefore decided accordingly by the lower courts.

The Supreme Court can hear and decide on fewer than ten percent of the more than a thousand cases that ask for hearing. But who is to decide what cases shall be heard? The rule is that when any four justices agree to grant a petition for *certiorari*—as these appeals for hearing are known in legal jargon—the Court will hear arguments in the case and decide it. But each of these petitions involves a brief asking the Court to hear the case, another brief asking the Court not to hear it and, likely as not, a record of all the legal proceedings in the lower courts.

Somebody has to read all this, digest it, and put it into simple and easily read form for the justices before they can decide whether to hear a case or not. That's where those eighteen young law clerks come in. This mass of petitions is split up amongst them. Each clerk then writes a summary or memorandum for his justice. This summary ostensibly states the facts of the case, the law on which the lower courts depended in deciding it, a short statement of previous cases on the same point and—finally— *a recommendation by the clerk that the case be heard or not heard by the Court.*

It is then up to the justice, of course, to decide whether he will accept or reject his clerk's recommendation. But we can see how easy it would be for a young law clerk, fresh from the groves of academe, where he was filled with a burning desire to remake America into the bright new socialist mold, to let at least some of his zeal creep into his recommendation.

There is an indication of how potent this influence has been in the fact that, in late 1957, the Harvard *Law Review* found that the Warren Supreme Court was falling badly behind in its docket of cases. The thing that was causing the trouble was that the Court was agreeing to hear an unprecedented number of cases. In the 1956–1957 term, for instance, it agreed to hear 208 cases. From 1948 to 1955, the figure ran from eighty-eight to 162 cases per term. Legal experts familiar with the Court's work said it deserved no sympathy for the jam into which it had got itself. It was busy putting its "liberal" hand on a whole batch of lower court decisions on the assumption that these courts didn't know what they were doing. It would be interesting if we could have another survey of how much these bright young law clerks had to do with the high court's determination to make the lower courts truly "inferior."

But we need no longer be in any doubt as to the power wielded by these workers behind the scenes. Congressman Gordon H. Scherer of Ohio, a member of the House Committee on Un-American Activities, had noted the influences under which these recent graduates had come in their college years. A number of college professors had been called before his committee. Congressman Scherer said:

Our committee hearings have disclosed a considerable amount of ill-will, bordering in some cases on hatred, by many professors for congressional investigating committees. They have determined in one way or another to destroy these committees ever since some of their clique were subpoenaed to tell about their communist and communist-front activities.

As a member of a congressional investigating committee, Congressman Scherer was especially interested in reading carefully some of the Supreme Court's decisions affecting the rights of congressional committees. He said:

I have read in some of the recent shocking Supreme Court decisions almost the exact words, phrases and arguments that have been used by some of these professors in their attacks against the committees.

Congressman Scherer suggested that these words and phrases very well might have crept into the decisions of the learned justices via some of those professors' former pupils, now hidden behind the bench of the highest court in the land.

Thanks to the enterprise of the weekly news magazine *U.S. News & World Report,* we have had an even more authoritative statement of the role of those bright young law clerks from one of their own number. *U.S. News* hunted up a former law clerk to Justice Jackson—William H. Rehnquist, now with a law firm in Phoenix, Arizona. In its issue of December 13, 1957, *U.S. News & World Report* printed the following words* from Mr. Rehnquist:

The bias of the clerks, in my opinion, is not a random or hit-and-miss bias. From my observations of two sets of Court clerks during the 1951 and 1952 terms, the political and legal prejudices of the clerks were by no means representative of the country as a whole nor of the Court which they served.

After conceding a wide diversity of opinion among the clerks themselves, and further conceding the difficulties and possible inaccuracies inherent in political cataloguing of people, it is nonetheless fair to say that the political cast of the clerks as a group was to the "left" of either the nation or the Court.

Some of the tenets of the "liberal" point of view which commanded the sympathy of a majority of the clerks I knew were: extreme solicitude for the claims of Communists and other criminal defendants, expansion of federal power at the expense of State power, great

---

* Reprinted from *U. S. News & World Report,* an independent weekly news magazine published at Washington. Copyright (1957) United States News Publishing Corporation.

sympathy toward any government regulation of business—in short, the political philosophy now espoused by the Court under Chief Justice Earl Warren.

And Mr. Rehnquist frankly added:

I cannot speak for any clerk other than myself in stating as a fact that unconscious bias *did* creep into his work. Looking back, I must admit that I was not guiltless on this score, and I greatly doubt if many of my fellow clerks were much less guiltless than I. And where such bias did have any effect, because of the political outlook of the group of clerks that I knew, its direction would be to the political "left."

We may be sure the situation is no better today—and may, indeed, be a great deal worse, as Congressman Scherer discovered in the parroting of words of leftist professors by the justices of the Supreme Court.

But, you say, what is the Court to do? The justices have to have clerks and they naturally choose those they think will be in sympathy with their views. Perhaps. But bear this in mind. These clerks are government employees. Their pay ranges from $5,500 to $6,500 a year—paid not by the justices but by the American taxpayer. And they are in a class by themselves as government employees. Unlike most others, the eighteen bright young men who serve as law clerks to the justices of the Supreme Court *are not subject to the regular government security or loyalty checks.*

# CHAPTER TWENTY

## *The Last Bastion Is Stormed*

In the years following the segregation decision—and particularly in the last year or two—the Warren Supreme Court struck down practically every bulwark we have raised against the communist conspiracy in America. In doing so, it continued to wipe out state lines and actually to leave the sovereign states helpless in the face of subversion. The examples given at the beginning of this book are only a few of the many decisions that have fallen from this revolutionary tribunal like manna for all those who would wreck our form of government.

The shape of things to come was indicated in 1955, when the Warren Court decided a case involving Dr. John P. Peters. Dr. Peters had a long pro-communist record. He also had a government job. When a question arose as to his loyalty to the government—and to the American taxpayers who were paying his salary—a loyalty board in the department in which he worked looked him over and decided he was all right. But his case had to go for final decision to a loyalty review board. It apparently made a much more thorough investigation of Dr. Peters, decided he was a loyalty risk—and ordered him out of his government job.

Dr. Peters (who has since died) took the case to the Supreme Court. *It cleared him* by declaring that the loyalty review board had no right to reverse the findings of a lower board—on what grounds nobody has been able to figure out clearly. Presumably only the Supreme Court can indulge in the reversal of findings as it suits the members' own peculiar conception of what is loyalty and what is not. The decision (Peters v. Hobby) was written—or at least delivered—by Chief Justice Warren, with Justices Black, Frankfurter, Minton, Clark, and Harlan concurring. Only Justices Reed and Burton dissented.

A year later, in the spring of 1956, the Warren Court struck a crippling blow (Pennsylvania v. Nelson) to the power of the sovereign American states to protect themselves against sedition. In so doing, it also continued to dip its busy fingers into the affairs of the states in direct contravention of the Constitution of the United States. Steve Nelson was an admitted leader of the Communist Party. He was considered by some as perhaps the most dangerous communist official in the country. The State of Pennsylvania had an antisedition law and in 1952 it convicted Nelson under that law and sentenced him to 20 years in prison.

Once again, President Eisenhower's Chief Justice, Earl Warren, was on tap to protect the "rights" of the leftists and communists. He issued a decision which literally wiped out the antisedition laws of forty-two states

—and freed Steve Nelson from the Pennsylvania conviction. The Chief Justice did this on the fantastic grounds that a federal law covered sedition and that therefore the state laws were null and void. He so held despite the fact that Congress, in passing the federal law, had no intention whatever of interfering with the state laws. Just how fantastic were these grounds for wiping out the states' protection against sedition, we will see in a moment when we come to that federal law which Chief Justice Warren said gave the states all the protection they needed. In freeing Steve Nelson, Warren had the concurrence of all his colleagues save Justices Reed, Burton, and Minton.

This decision had some strange repercussions, which may well lead us to ask if the real "reasoning" behind it did not perhaps hark back to the Court's action in the school segregation cases. The question comes to mind because of some facts revealed by the Senate Sub-Committee on Internal Security (*Hearings,* October 28-29, 1957)—facts which were reported in few, if any, Northern newspapers.

State law-enforcement officers in Kentucky were extremely troubled about increasing communist activity in their state, particularly around Louisville. It seemed to head up in a man named Braden. Whether he was an actual communist or not had not been proved. But, in any case, he and his wife bought a house in a suburb of Louisville in a neighborhood where only white families live. A day or two later, they transferred the house to a colored family. Whether the colored family were communists or just innocent dupes is not indicated. But before they moved into the house, they asked for police protection. The local police refused, on the ground that nothing had been brought to their attention to indicate there would be any trouble. It later transpired that the house was a virtual arsenal, loaded with power rifles, shotguns, and pistols.

Shortly thereafter, a white man with a communist record turned up at the house. He said he had come to "guard" it. A portable radio was placed under the house and a little after midnight one night the house was blown up. The state and local authorities had two theories to go on. One, of course, was that the white people in the neighborhood wanted to chase the colored family out. The other was that the whole thing had been communist-planned and inspired. Every one of the white neighbors submitted readily to questioning by the police and other state authorities, and every one of them voluntarily took a lie-detector test. They all passed it with flying colors. But when the authorities questioned the "guard" and other suspected communists, they took the Fifth Amendment —refusing to answer on the ground that their answers might incriminate them. They called the investigation of the blowing up of the house a "witch hunt." They refused to take lie-detector tests.

The authorities placed what evidence they had before a grand jury, which investigated further. It then brought in an indictment against Braden and five others for criminal sedition. The grand jury acted under the Kentucky sedition law which was almost as old as the State of Kentucky itself and the legality of which had never before been questioned. Braden was tried in the courts of Kentucky, found guilty as charged, and sentenced to ten years in prison and a five-thousand-dollar fine. The indictments against the other five were pending when the Supreme Court, speaking through Chief Justice Warren, issued its decision in the Nelson case, in which it wiped out all the state laws against sedition.

The State of Kentucky then was forced to free Carl Braden, who had been convicted of sedition by a jury of his peers, and it had to drop the indictments against his five cohorts.

One week after issuing the Nelson decision, the Supreme Court came up with another one on April 9, 1956. It is known as the Slochower case, and by its decision in this case the Court took away from the states and cities the right to fire a teacher in *tax-supported* schools who refuses to reveal his communist connections. You pay the taxes. You send your youngsters to the schools these taxes build and support. You also pay the teachers. You expect them to teach to your children, besides all the other things they must learn, the fundamentals of American government and life. But the Supreme Court of the United States says you have no right to fire a teacher—whom you pay—when he refuses to reveal his connection with a conspiracy that hates and despises every inherent principle of Americanism.

Harry Slochower was a teacher in Brooklyn College— a free, tax-supported institution in one of the boroughs of New York City. The City has had a law on its books since 1938 which requires that any teacher in its public schools or colleges who is called before an investigating committee and hides behind the Fifth Amendment in order to conceal his communist connections is automatically fired. That is what happened in the case of Slochower. He was called before an investigating committee, asked about his extensive pro-communist record, and, in answer to each question on this score, hid behind the Fifth Amendment and refused to answer. The Board of Higher Education, which administers Brooklyn College for the City of New York, fired him. But the Supreme Court, speaking this time through Justice Tom Clark, ordered the Board of Higher Education to reinstate Slochower in his job and *give him $40,000 in back pay.*

Justice Clark had the concurrence of Chief Justice Warren and Justices Frankfurter, Black, and Douglas. In this case, there were four dissents—by Justices Reed, Burton, and Minton, the three who had also dissented in the Nelson case, and by Justice Harlan.

But Justice Harlan didn't stay off the reservation for long. One month later he was back in the camp of his "liberal" colleagues with a decision (Cole v. Young) that has broken down the government's own security program. Justice Harlan and his colleagues—with the exception of Justices Reed, Clark, and Minton—evidently "reasoned" that to hold a government job is some sort of inherent "right" on which every left-wing troublemaker has a claim. The rights of all other Americans, without whose sufferance—and taxes—there would be no government jobs, did not seem to concern Justices Harlan, Black, Douglas, Frankfurter, Warren, and Burton. The taxpayers, to the justices' way of thinking, have no right to demand that the employees they hire to run the government should not jeopardize the security of that government.

The justices, of course, could not declare boldly that it is all right to keep a communist or a drunkard, let us say, in the secret laboratory of the Atomic Energy Commission. So they did the next best thing. Speaking through Justice Harlan, they said that security risks employed by government bureaus—and paid by American taxpayers —could not be dismissed unless they were in so-called "sensitive" positions. It seems not to have occurred to the justices that a government position of any type is a position of trust and that any government's existence is jeopardized which cannot trust its own employees—no matter what position they hold. This decision has resulted in the restoration to their jobs in the government service of at least 300 security risks!

But Justice Harlan did not let the matter rest here. A year after this decision, he wrote still another (Service v. Dulles), involving the dismissal from the State Department of a man named John Stewart Service. Service was one of that group of State Department employees, which also included in the top echelon Dean Acheson and General George Marshall, who were knowingly or unknowingly doing the bidding of the communist-dominated Institute of Pacific Relations in delivering China into the hands of the communists. But Service's record proved too much even for Dean Acheson and he finally felt called upon to drop Service from the State Department.

Service had been mixed up in the very smelly *Amerasia* case, which came up in 1945, while we were still at war.

*Amerasia* was a magazine set up by the IPR and edited by a communist, Philip Jaffe. The FBI found in its offices 1,700 secret government documents—one of them, for instance, dealing with something called "A-bomb" and marked "top secret." *Amerasia* and its editor, Jaffe, came into possession of these documents from a number of sources. But the FBI discovered John Stewart Service visiting Jaffe's hotel room and turning over to him State Department documents which he warned Jaffe were secret. Service later admitted he had made copies of documents which came into his hands during the course of his State Department work and turned these copies over to Jaffe.

All this meant nothing to Justice Harlan. He ordered John Stewart Service restored to a job in the State Department and, at this writing, there he is—at a nice increase in pay. The decision of the Supreme Court in this case—on June 17, 1957—was 8 to 0. Justice Clark took no part because he had been in the Attorney-General's office when the *Amerasia* case arose.

Hardly a week went by during the spring 1957 session of the Warren Supreme Court that a new crack was not hammered into the wall we had raised against the communist conspiracy. Through those cracks the communist termites are now happily swarming. In January the Court ordered a new trial for Ben Gold, a labor leader who had been convicted of perjury because he lied when he took the non-communist oath required by the Taft-Hartley Act. While Gold was being tried, the FBI contacted several members of the jury on another and entirely unrelated case. *The FBI agents were not even aware that the jurors*

*were sitting in the Gold case.* But the Court, always solicitous for the rights of communists, said this was an "official intrusion into the privacy of the jury" and ordered
a new trial. The government threw up its hands in disgust
and dropped the case against Gold.

Then, in May, the Court arrogated to itself the functions of a State Bar Examining Board to say who could
and could not practice law before the state courts. A man
named Konigsberg applied for a license to practice law in
California. He came up before the State Bar Examining
Board. The Board must certify that an applicant is a
person of good moral character before he can be admitted to practice. The California Committee on Un-
American Activities in 1949 listed Konigsberg among
"notorious Stalinists who have consistently followed the
twists and turns of the Stalinist line." When he was called
before the House Committee on Un-American Activities
he hid behind the Fifth Amendment when asked about his
communist connections. The California Bar Examining
Board, in the face of this record, asked him a simple
question: "Are you a communist?" He wouldn't give a
direct answer, but went into a spiel about "nameless in-
formers." One such was a woman—who did not hesitate
to give her name—who, in Konigsberg's presence, testi-
fied that she knew him to be a communist. He was asked
if he cared to deny her statement. He twisted and turned
and dodged answering. The State Bar Examining Board
refused to grant him permission to practice law before
the California courts. Not so, the Supreme Court of
the United States. Speaking through Justice Black
(Konigsberg v. State Bar), it ordered the sovereign State

of California to admit him to its bar. Justice Black actually said the California Board could not draw inferences of doubtful "character and loyalty" because a man won't say whether he belongs to the Communist Party! Thus the Court seized from California and every other state in the Union the right to say that the members of the communist conspiracy, who hate all American law, shall not be permitted to practice it before their courts. It's that same law, incidentally, that the justices of the Supreme Court take a sworn oath to uphold.

The Court topped off these decisions with one (Sentner v. Barton) canceling the deportation of a communist because "the Justice Department lacks authority to ban communist activity by an alien who has been under a deportation order for six months"—despite the fact that an act of Congress (the McCarran-Walter Immigration Act) conferred that authority. Fast on the heels of this came Justice Brennan's decision opening the FBI files to all and sundry.

# CHAPTER TWENTY-ONE

# Red Monday

But on June 17, 1957, the Court really went to town
—amid the cheers and hurrahs of the communist conspirators. The day has come to be known as Red Monday, as well it might. It was on that day that Chief Justice Warren, with Justices Frankfurter, Black, Douglas,
Harlan, and Brennan concurring—and only Justice
Clark dissenting*—took away from congressional investigating committees their freedom of inquiry. It did so (in
Watkins v. U.S.) on the ground that a witness who refused to answer questions wasn't in contempt of Congress
if the committee failed to spell out for him the "pertinence" of its questions and the purpose of the inquiry.
As pointed out in the beginning of this book, congressional committees investigate to get needed information
for their constituents and to write necessary legislation.
But, according to Chief Justice Warren, who read the decision, they now have to know what they are going to do

* Justices Burton and Whittaker did not participate in this case.

and how to do it—and explain it all explicitly to witnesses—before they can get the information they need to decide how they are going to act. That may sound ridiculous to a normal mind, but that's what the Court said.

In the process, the Court also nailed down the clamp it had placed—in the Slochower decision—on the rights of the states to protect their students against subversive teachers. Paul M. Sweezy, a professor at the University of New Hampshire, was accused of teaching communist doctrine to his students. The legislature of the sovereign State of New Hampshire directed its attorney-general to find out if this was true. He tried on two separate occasions to get some information out of Sweezy. Sweezy denied he had ever been a member of the Communist Party. But he would not answer any questions about his alleged connections with known communists. The highest court of the State of New Hampshire held Sweezy in contempt. The Supreme Court reversed the New Hampshire court and freed Sweezy. Why? Well, the learned justices couldn't quite decide. Chief Justice Warren and three of his colleagues (Justices Douglas, Black, and Harlan) said, in effect, the state had gone about the whole matter the wrong way. Justice Frankfurter said, in a separate concurrence, that state officials have no right to question the beliefs and associations of professors in state institutions! You build buildings for them to teach in; you hire them; you pay them—but don't you dare ask if they are good Americans! Justices Burton and Clark dissented from this opinion; Justices Brennan and Whittaker took no part.

It was on that same Red Monday that Justice

Harlan delivered the decision*—with the help of Justices Black, Frankfurter, Douglas, Warren, and Burton —which makes it practically impossible to prosecute conspirators against America until they physically start overthrowing the government. The decision involved the Smith Act, which makes it a crime "to advocate and teach the duty and necessity of overthrowing the Government of the United States by force and violence." In 1951 the Court under Chief Justice Vinson, by a 6-2 vote, upheld the constitutionality of the Smith Act and cited the communist conspiracy in America as a "clear and present danger." But now the Warren Court has said, with some hair-splitting that would put a "Philadelphia lawyer" to shame, that the "clear and present danger" is an abstract principle. In effect, it doesn't become concrete until guns are fired and bombs thrown.

You will recall that, in the Steve Nelson case, the Court, through Chief Justice Warren, wiped out the anti-sedition laws of 42 states on the ground that we had a federal law covering the matter. What do you suppose that federal law was? It was this Smith Act, which Justice Harlan and his colleagues, *including Chief Justice Warren,* now practically nullified—the law which Warren had said earlier gave the states all the protection they needed against sedition!

Thus the Warren Court wound up its 1956–1957 session. In the three years up to and including that term— three years with Mr. Eisenhower's Chief Justice at the head of the Court—it issued at least fifteen decisions designed to put the meddling fingers of the federal politi-

* Yates v. U.S.

cians further into state affairs, and to break down completely all our defenses against the communist conspirators in our midst. Chief Justice Warren wrote five of these decisions and concurred in all fifteen. Justice Harlan wrote three of the decisions. Justice Brennan wrote one. Justice Harlan dissented in only two of the fifteen cases. That is the record of the Eisenhower appointees to the Court. Of the remaining decisions, Justice Black wrote two, Justice Clark one, and three were unsigned. All fifteen were concurred in by Justices Frankfurter, Douglas, and Black, as well as by Chief Justice Warren. In other words, the Chief Justice has aligned himself completely with the leftist members of the Court. There were five dissents by Justice Reed, five by Justice Burton, and three by Justice Minton. But Reed and Minton are no longer on the Court, thus leaving as almost the only dissenter Justice Clark, who filed eight disagreements—some of them excoriating his fellow justices for impliedly giving aid and comfort to the communist enemy.

In the first part of the 1957–1958 session, still in progress as this is being written, the justices did nothing to soften the deep-red hue of this record. In December, 1957, they stopped the deportation of another alien with a communist record, though Congress has declared that aliens with past communist records must be sent back to the country of their origin. Justice Frankfurter wrote the decision and was joined by Black, Douglas, and Brennan. Justice Clark wasn't so lonesome this time in his dissent—he had the company of Harlan, Burton, Clark, and Whittaker, though Justice Harlan made sure to signify that he was dissenting "with regret."

The Court's solicitude for communists and criminals was further illustrated in the fall of 1957 when it gave its blessing to a convicted felon in California who failed to fulfill the requirements of a state law requiring registration with the police. According to the Court, the felon was within his "rights" because he didn't know about the law. For law-abiding American citizens, ignorance of the law is no excuse for breaking it. Witness, for instance, the raft of traffic tickets handed out every day for violations of rules broken by ignorant motorists. But, according to the Supreme Court, convicted felons are in a class by themselves. Justice Douglas, for the Court, admitted that "ignorance of the law will not excuse" but that in the felon's case, the conduct "was wholly passive—mere failure to register!"

# CHAPTER TWENTY-TWO

# Your Job, Your Business, Your Estate —and Murder

But it is not only in its softness on the Red conspiracy that the Warren Supreme Court has played so skillfully into the hands of the socialist revolutionaries in America. Along with this has gone a continuation of the practice of the Roosevelt-packed Court in taking from the states and their citizens control over their own resources and their own livelihood. And the Court has not hesitated even to tell an American citizen the manner in which his estate must be disposed of after he dies—no matter what his will says. The Court has even handed (I know this is hard to believe, but it is true) a new "charter of liberty" to murderers and rapists.

In 1954, the Court seized (in Phillips Petroleum v. Wisconsin) from the southwestern states control of natural-gas production and handed it to the federal bureaucrats in Washington. Today it is natural gas; tomorrow it could be your corner filling station or grocery store—or local newspaper.

In 1957, the Warren Court ordered the duPont Company to divest itself of the stock it held in the General Motors Corporation. This was hailed by all the "liberals" as a great "antimonopoly" decision, though none of them has yet explained how one corporation has a "monopoly" over another when it owns less than 25 percent of its stock. They haven't explained either just what is the "monopoly" General Motors enjoys as it engages in terrific competition with several other great motor companies, and a number of smaller ones, to sell its products.

In the duPont decision (U.S. v. E. I. duPont de Nemours Co.), the Court went its merry way ignoring the language and purpose of the original law (the Clayton Anti-Trust Act), forty years of administrative rules by the Federal Trade Commission in administering it, and all other precedents except one District Court decision. Justice Burton, who dissented, even charged his colleagues with applying the wrong section of the law to the case and declared: "The Court cites no authority in support of its new interpretation of this 40-year-old statute."

The decision was reminiscent of Justice Frankfurter's declaration years earlier that an elevator operator running his elevator up and down in a building was crossing state lines and so was in "interstate" commerce. The Clayton Act applied to what are known as "horizontal" stock acquisitions—those by which a company buys stock in a competing company—but not to "vertical" acquisitions, whereby a company buys stock in another one which is not a competitor. The duPont Company, chemical manufacturers, obviously is not in competition with General Motors, automobile manufacturers. But, as one legal cynic put it, there was nothing surprising about the Court's decision: "It was neither illogical nor unexpected that this Supreme Court could declare that horizontal and vertical mean the same thing. The Supreme Court has done it before."

The Warren Supreme Court, of course, has not ignored the labor field either. In 1956, Mr. Justice Douglas wrote an opinion (Ry. Employees Dept. v. Hanson), concurred in by the entire Court, ordering three citizens of the sovereign State of Nebraska to join a union if they wanted to keep their jobs. Thus the Court capped a whole series of previous decisions establishing over the rank-and-file of American workers what Donald Richberg has so aptly called the "Labor Union Monopoly."

In 1957, another unanimous decision (Penna. v. Bd. of Directors of City Trusts)—an unsigned one—did away at one fell swoop with a principle which has been imbedded in our law since the beginning of the Republic. It is a principle governing charitable trusts and has to do with the right of any American to dispose of his private property for the benefit of anybody he chooses.

There is a school in Philadelphia called Girard College. It never has been, and is not now, supported by public funds of any kind. The college is 125 years old. It was set up to fulfill the specifications of the will of Stephen Girard, a wealthy Philadelphian. The college always has been supported by a trust fund set up by Girard in his will. The trust fund, under wise administration, is now somewhere in the neighborhood of a hundred million dollars, and the school itself takes care of about a thousand youngsters a year. In his will, Stephen Girard

directed that the bulk of his estate be put into a perpetual
trust and the trust was directed, also in his will, to set
up and maintain "a school for poor white orphan boys."
That is what the trust has done for 125 years.

But, you say, what has the Supreme Court to do with
all this? Hasn't a man a right to dispose of his money any
way he chooses? And wasn't Girard carrying out a noble
and humane purpose in leaving his fortune for the education of poor white orphan boys who might not otherwise
have the advantages he provided?

Well, let us see what happened. You will learn quickly
how far our Supreme Court is willing to go in its lawless-
ness. In order to be certain that the provisions of such
wills and trusts as Stephen Girard's are carried out according to the donors' wishes, the City of Philadelphia
did what many other states and cities have done for the
protection of its citizens. It named a Board of Directors
of City Trusts—a board of trustees—to carry out the
terms of wills and estates left in perpetual trust in that
city. Of the fourteen members on the board, twelve were
named by the Court of Common Pleas. The other two
were *ex officio* members—one the president of the City
Council and the other the city's mayor. This is similar to
the practice in many states where private institutions of
various types operate under a state charter and the governor of the state is named an *ex officio* member of the
board of trustees or directors.

In 1954, two Negroes tried to gain admission to Girard
College. The Board of Trustees turned them down because, under Girard's will—of which they were the trustees—they could admit to the college only "poor white

orphans." In fact, a clause in the will stated that, if the trustees administered the fund in any way other than that specified in the will, the money would be forfeited—which, of course, meant the college would close down.

The two Negroes took the case to court, and the highest court of the State of Pennsylvania upheld the Board of Trustees, stating emphatically that "it is one of our most fundamental legal principles" that an American citizen has a right to dispose of his own property in any way he sees fit, and that this right is so inherent and so protected that it must be enforced no matter how much others may disapprove of it. The Pennsylvania Supreme Court said specifically: "He [the man who makes a will] is entitled to his idiosyncrasies and even to his prejudices."

At least that was the case until a packed Supreme Court started legislating for Americans. The lawyers for the two Negroes asked the Supreme Court for a writ of *certiorari*—for the Court to hear arguments in the case and decide it. Attorneys for the Board of Trustees, of course, opposed this plea. There were no arguments on the merits of the case, but the Court agreed to accept it *on its merits*. Would it not be interesting if we could have a look at the memoranda and recommendations on this petition by some of those "bright young men" we have previously considered, through whose hands all such pleas must pass?

In a brief unsigned opinion, to which there were no dissents, the Supreme Court reversed the Pennsylvania high court and declared Girard College must admit the Negroes because, even though the Board of Trustees was acting as a trustee for the Girard trust fund, it "is an agency of the State of Pennsylvania" and therefore its refusal to admit the Negroes amounts to "discrimination by the State." The Supreme Court so declared, despite the fact that the lower court pointed out that Girard's will "was never administered by the City in its governmental or sovereign capacity." It was administered by the Board "solely in the capacity of a fiduciary or trustee, governed, bound and limited by the directions and provisions of Girard's will."

The Board's attorneys, following the Supreme Court's unsigned five-and-a-half-line decision, asked for a rehearing on the merits of the case. The Court summarily refused it. What were they afraid of? That argument by competent attorneys would force them to reverse themselves?

The incalculable harm possible from this decision of the Court—depriving the free American of his right to dispose of his estate as he chooses—can be seen from the words of the Pennsylvania high court. It pointed out that private trusts for charitable purposes "abound in overwhelming numbers." Then it said:

> We have charitable trusts for ministers of various church denominations, for foreign missions, for churches, priests, Catholics, Protestants, Jews, whites, Negroes, for relief of the Indians, for widows or orphan children of Masons or other fraternities, for sectarian old-folks homes, orphanages and so on.

Certainly no one would contend that a donor or testator could not establish a charity, the beneficiaries of which were to be those whom he designated—persons of any prescribed race, creed or color, or however otherwise differentiated.

Maybe "no one would contend" so, but the Supreme Court of the United States not only contends but says its ruling is the law.

You may think that in this long string of decisions, the Supreme Court has gone about as far as it can go. But you would be mistaken. One of the chief reasons why free men set up governments is to protect the majority of decent, law-abiding citizens amongst them against the minority of those who insist on living without the law. Absence of government in such a case means anarchy. Now, you say, certainly you are not going to accuse the Supreme Court of trying to bring about a condition of anarchy. No, I'm not. I simply ask you to draw your own conclusion after reading the facts in the following case.

In 1954, in Washington, D.C., a woman was doing her washing in the laundry room in the basement of her apartment house. A man named Mallory, with a mask over his face, went into the laundry room and attacked and raped the woman. The police were called, and the next day they brought Mallory, who lived in the janitor's quarters of the apartment house, into the police station for questioning. He agreed to take a lie-detector test and then said he wanted to talk. He made a complete confession of the crime. Even when faced with the woman against whom he committed the crime, he again repeated his confession. He had been brought to the police station at first only as a suspect—the police did not have sufficient evidence on which to go before a magistrate and have

him arraigned. His confession came only seven hours
after his arrest. He was indicted, tried, and found guilty,
and the jury recommended the death penalty. Mallory
never contended that any force, threats, promises, or coer-
cion were used to get his confession. But he appealed
his conviction on the ground of illegal detention and un-
necessary delay in arraignment.

The United States Court of Appeals in Washington
threw out his contention for what it was—an obvious
subterfuge to get a confessed rapist off the hook—and
said his conviction should stand. But his lawyer appealed
the case to the Supreme Court.

Justice Frankfurter (in Mallory v. U.S.), for a
unanimous Court, did not find Mallory innocent of rape,
though Justice Frankfurter referred to him tenderly as a
"19 year old lad." The Court did not even suggest there
was any doubt about his guilt. But it made a new rule.
It said the police had no right to question a suspect
before arraignment. Since the police *had* questioned him
—and got a confession with no hint whatever of any
"third-degree" methods—the Court ordered that he was
to have a new trial. Whereupon the prosecuting attorney
threw up his hands, declaring that the wording of the
Court's decision made it impossible to retry the case with
any hope of conviction. The rapist Mallory walks the
streets today a free man—free to rape again—thanks to
the Supreme Court of the United States.

The chief of the Justice Department's criminal division
has said that the Mallory decision "clearly demonstrates
that a great many very serious crimes will go unpunished
. . . not because the truth cannot be ascertained, but

because of the procedures that have to be followed
to develop the facts." He went on: "The place where
the impact of this decision will be greatest is in the gang-
ster crimes. It is the real hardened professional criminals
who will take advantage of this."

The Washington *Evening Star* quoted a proponent of
this fantastic decision as explaining it this way: "Police
can question people if they want to be questioned as long
as they are free agents. A suspect can be brought to
headquarters and questioned as long as he is free to
walk out at any time. But as soon as he is under arrest, it
is 'unreasonable delay' in arraigning him if police use any
time to make a case against him." As Senator William
E. Jenner pointed out on the floor of the Senate, this
means that "a suspect cannot be questioned *before* his arrest unless he agrees, and *if he is arrested* he cannot be
questioned *afterwards.*"

The results of this decision are already being felt in
many places. A man confessed to murdering a girl. He
was convicted and sentenced to death. But an appeals
court was obliged to say, under the Supreme Court's new
rule, that the confession can't be validly used because
there was too long an interval—sixteen hours—between
arrest and arraignment.

In Washington, Chief of Police Robert V. Murray
pointed to another Eastern case involving the rape and
murder of an eight-year-old girl. Thirty detectives were at
work on the case. Over a thousand people were questioned about the crime. But, said Chief Murray, "What
good will it do to bring in a good suspect, question him,
and get a confession if this decision stands? This deci-

sion says he must be arraigned immediately and not questioned after we arrest him."

And Chief Murray put his finger on the Court's overpowering concern for the rights of the criminal while the rest of our law-abiding citizens can go hang. He said: "Innocent persons in great numbers would, of necessity, have to be arraigned and the stigma of a police record placed against them unless there is reasonable time to clear them by interrogation and investigation before arraignment." But to the "liberal" Supreme Court, so very much concerned about the "civil liberties" of communists and criminals, this means nothing.

# CHAPTER TWENTY-THREE

# The Communists' Jubilation
# —and a Warning

In the light of this whole sorry record of the Court's usurpation of the rights of the states and the citizens, and the terrifying go-ahead signal it has given to the communist conspiracy in America, we need not be surprised at the jubilation in communist circles over the Supreme Court of the United States.

The Court's decision in the Smith Act case freed from conviction fourteen West Coast communists. Dorothy Healey Connolly, former chairman of the Communist Party in Los Angeles County and spokesman for the communists on the West Coast, rejoiced: "This is the greatest victory the Communist Party ever had." She added that it would "result in the rejuvenation of the Communist Party in America." It certainly has, because, as a result of the Court's rulings, one communist after another has been set free by the lower courts; to say nothing of a whole batch of fellow-traveling leftists who

143

thumb their noses at congressional committees and are free from punishment—thanks to the Supreme Court of the United States.

The communist *Daily Worker* in New York carried ecstatic front-page headlines about the Court's decisions. It hailed them as "liberty rulings" and "A Milestone for Democracy." The communists even held a rally in September, 1957. Its purpose? Let the *Daily Worker* spell it out: *"To pay honor to the U.S. Supreme Court and its recent decisions,"* and to *"Hit out at attempts to undo the decisions."*

We may well ask if Messrs. Warren, Frankfurter, Black, Douglas, Harlan, and Brennan are proud of these encomiums from the enemies of the nation whose laws these justices are sworn to uphold. Even so restrained and objective an observer as David Lawrence has called the Court's decisions "Treason's Greatest Victory." Those are strong words—words we should think would bring at least a few sleepless nights to any justice who has still left in his soul a scrap of love for the American Republic.

We might ponder well—as might also the justices of the Supreme Court—the words of one who knows, perhaps better than anybody else in America, whereof he speaks. Robert Morris was the counsel of the Senate Sub-Committee on Internal Security. His knowledge of the communist conspiracy in the United States can be matched perhaps only by that of J. Edgar Hoover. Morris was an officer in Naval Intelligence and has had years of service with the Internal Security Committee. He also has a thorough knowledge of the law. In fact, he was elected a judge in New York and resigned that post to return to his work with the Internal Security Committee because of his concern over the inroads the communist conspiracy was making in the country he loved. Judge Morris is not a headline hunter nor an amateur investigator. His investigation of the Institute of Pacific Relations was a model of careful fact finding and considerate handling of witnesses and resulted in an unassailable record of the work of the communist-dominated IPR in influencing the American government to let China fall into the hands of the communists. Here is what Judge Robert Morris had to say about the Supreme Court of the United States:

*An aggressive majority of the Supreme Court, bypassing judicial precedent and grievously misunderstanding the nature of the Soviet organization in the United States, has undertaken a campaign to level all existing barriers against communist penetration.* This majority has denied to the states the right to protect themselves against communist insurrection and infiltration on the theory that Congress has preempted that function for the federal government. Ironically enough, it has supplemented that decree by eliminating for all practical purposes the right of the federal government to check subversion and insurrection.

The spectacle of five judges, in the face of this world struggle, by-passing established judicial precedent and forcing the FBI to expose its secret and complicated files to the sworn enemies of this country is difficult to comprehend.

So it is. But perhaps, now that we have had a look at the judges themselves, their past records, and the purpose for which they were packed onto the Court, we can see a little more clearly the frightening role they were expected to play. It amounted to nothing less than to break down the sovereignty of the American states, to bring all power over the states and their citizens to the center, and to give the enemies of America a free hand in their efforts to destroy the American republic and set up in its place a collectivist society. We must admit that the justices, in most cases, have played their roles like veteran actors.

# CHAPTER TWENTY-FOUR

# *To Turn the Tide*

But all those who are devoted to our American way of life and who believe it is worth saving against the encroachments of the collectivist sappers are agreed that, if it is to survive, something must be done about the Supreme Court.

A number of proposals have been made—and undoubtedly more will be made in the future—for dealing with this great crisis in our history. The major ones so far put forth are listed here, with a brief explanation or discussion of the points involved, so that Americans will know what they are and be able to think intelligently about them and about the overriding problem of our times with which they are meant to deal.

First, of course, is the constitutional provision which states that any official of the United States "shall be removed from office on impeachment for, and conviction of, treason, bribery, or other high crimes and misdemeanors." The Constitution also provides that judges

147

"shall hold their office during good behavior." The impeachment process, of course, is a long, difficult, and cumbersome one and has been used only a very few times in our history. Yet it is well for us to remember that it is there—to be used whenever the charges are such as to justify a trial for impeachment by the Senate, whose members are the representatives of the sovereign states; and, let us add, whenever the sovereign states and their citizens—who in the end constitute the ultimate jury—give their backing to the senators who represent them in what is, at best, a difficult proceeding.

The next group of proposals has to do with the appointment, tenure, qualifications, and service of the justices themselves. There are four of these proposals:

First: That a limit—four, six, or ten years—be placed on the terms of Supreme Court justices. At present, the justices are appointed to serve "during good behavior," which generally has meant for life. But congressmen, senators, even the President, serve for fixed terms. Why, it is asked, should not the justices?

Second: That justices be reconfirmed by the Senate at stated intervals. This proposal was first made by David Lawrence. At present, the justices are confirmed only once—when first named to the bench. Mr. Lawrence's suggestion would give the Senate a check on the justices, say every four years or so.

Third: That at least one of each two successive nominees to the Court should have had ten years of judicial experience. This proposal was first made by Senator John Stennis and has since been taken up by others. It stems from a startling discovery which the Senator made—that since 1932 the Court has departed on thirty-five occasions from decisions previously rendered, whereas there had been only twenty-nine such reversals in the entire history of the Court before 1932. In other words, in 143 years of its history the Court reversed previous decisions only twenty-nine times. But in just the last twenty-five years it has reversed previous decisions thirty-five times.

Fourth: That the President be deprived of the power of federal court appointments entirely and that the Senate should elect all federal judges.

It would seem that the adoption of the second proposal —that the justices be reconfirmed at stated intervals by the Senate—might do away with the necessity of the first one—placing a limit on their terms of office. It could be stated that if the Senate wished to give no reason for not reconfirming, no stigma would be attached to the lack of approval by the Senate. This would enable the Senate to drop a justice who, for instance, may have grown too old to carry on the work of the Court but who refuses to retire. And certain retirement benefits could be kept in force even for justices who could not pass muster with the Senate but who had not reached the retirement age. That would obviate any charge that the Senate was taking away a justice's livelihood in refusing to reconfirm him in his job on the Court.

But the major effect of both proposals—that justices serve fixed terms or stand for reconfirmation by the Senate, or both—would be on the justices themselves. It would take them out of the privileged class in which they are *answerable to no one* and place them where they belong as the public servants of a federal republic. They would become answerable to the representatives of the sovereign states, without which states there would be no federal republic—and no Supreme Court.

As to Senator Stennis's proposal that at least one of each two successive nominees to the Court should have had at least ten years of previous judicial experience, no one who has read thus far in this book could doubt the necessity for such a reform. If we apply some such rule to the members of the Supreme Court appointed since 1937, when packing began, we can see how far short they fall on judicial experience. There have been seventeen appointments since that time (including the Eisenhower appointees as of this writing). Their total previous judicial experience amounts to thirty-seven and a half years—and that includes Justice Black's eighteen months as a police-court judge and Justice Murphy's service on a City Recorder's court. If we assume that each should have had at least ten years of previous experience—a total of 170 years—we can see that our last seventeen justices have fallen short of that logical minimum by 132½ years.

In fact, it would seem that Senator Stennis's proposal does not go quite far enough—that *all* justices should be required to have had considerable previous judicial experience or that the exceptions should be at least highly eminent authorities on *constitutional* law.

It would also seem that at least part, if not all, of this previous experience should have been gained in service on the *highest courts of the states*, rather than solely in the federal judiciary. Many careful observers of our federal courts are of the opinion that they have reached their lowest level in recent years because of the long tenure in office of New Deal-Fair Deal-"Modern Republican" presidents. Certainly during the Roosevelt-Truman regimes many appointments to federal judgeships were made without regard to quality and chiefly on the basis of political expediency and reward.

Appointments or election to Supreme or Appellate courts in the states, on the other hand, generally go to men who have gained a well-earned reputation for legal and judicial sagacity among people who are able to watch them closely—the citizens of their own states. This is not to say, of course, that all state judges are of Supreme Court caliber or that all federal judges are not. But, generally speaking, the caliber of a man who has risen to a post on the highest court of his state is likely to be a good deal higher than that of a political hack who got a federal-court appointment because he voted "right" on this or that measure or delivered the precinct vote to the "right" presidential candidate. Also, a judge on a high state court is bound to be much more aware of the place of the sovereign states in our federal republic than is one who has served only on the federal courts.

This brings us to the fourth proposal in this group—that the President should be deprived entirely of all federal-court appointments—including those to the Supreme Court—and that the Senate should elect all federal judges. This will immediately raise the cry of "politics!"—the charge that such a reform will put all federal judgeships at the mercy of the political pulling and hauling in the Senate. We may well ask what they have been at the mercy of for the past two decades—if not the political machinations of presidents surrounded by social revolutionaries who would change our whole form of government and life?

In the case of federal judgeships below the Supreme Court level, had they been elected by the Senate in the past twenty years they would at least be a good deal more diversified as to political adherence than the presidential appointees. After all, we did have a few Senates in which the opposition to the president was in the majority.

As to Supreme Court appointments, could the Senate have done any worse than Messrs. Roosevelt, Truman, and Eisenhower? Certainly this is a proposal that should be carefully considered. Perhaps a wise course would be for the Senate to name two or three qualified men from among whom the President would have to make his choice. And this would be within the spirit of the Constitution, which says the President should make appointments to the Supreme Court *by and with the advice and consent* of the Senate.

This brings up, of course, the role of the Senate in the Supreme Court appointments of the past twenty years. There is no dodging the fact that, while our last three presidents have been busy packing the Court, the Senate of the United States has not been blameless. Had it so chosen, the Senate could have blocked any one of those appointments. There were bitter fights on some of them, but in the end the Senate went along and approved the appointments. This is one more evidence of the distance we have strayed from our traditional form of government. The senators, who are supposed to represent the sovereign states of the American Union, have been so busy appeasing an Executive with billions of dollars of taxpayers' money to dole out that they have in many cases forgotten why they are in Washington.

Nevertheless, in Supreme Court appointments up to now the Senate has been faced with more or less of a presidential *fait accompli*. Were the Senate itself to initiate the appointments, it could very well be a good deal more independent of the Executive, particularly if the members felt the pressure of an aroused constituency which was watching carefully the caliber of the men named to the highest court in the land.

Most, if not all, of the above proposals would require constitutional amendment. And they would not, of course, affect the Court as at present constituted. Neither of these is a good reason why they should not be pushed, since, if reform of the Court is needed—and we can no longer doubt that it is—some such action is of paramount importance for the future as well as now.

However, there are two other proposals which open the way to us to do something right now about the precarious constitutional crisis in which the packed Supreme Court has involved us.

The first of these is nearly as old as our government itself. It has been used on a number of occasions—both successfully and unsuccessfully—by the sovereign states. It is called "interposition" and has most recently been fully expounded by the brilliant young editor of the Richmond *News-Leader,* James Jackson Kilpatrick. Anyone interested in our past experiences with interposition could not do better than to read Mr. Kilpatrick's excellent volume *The Sovereign States: Notes of a Citizen of Virginia.*

Interposition is based on the Virginia Declaration of
1798, written by Thomas Jefferson and James Madison.
That resolution reads:

> In case of a deliberate, palpable, and dangerous exer
> cise of other powers not granted by the said compact
> [the Constitution], the States who are parties thereto,
> have the right, and are in duty bound, to interpose for
> arresting the progress of the evil, within their respec
> tive limits, the authorities, rights, and liberties apper
> taining to them.

What this means is that when the Executive or the
Court violates the Constitution by usurping powers which
the Constitution forbids, the states themselves—three
fourths of which form a power without which there would
be no Constitution and no federal government—must interpose to "arrest the progress of the evil" being committed by their own creature (the federal government)
and force it to conform to the body of laws (the Constitution) which the states set up to govern its conduct.

Interposition, of course, is within the power of the sovereign states, as states. Whether any single one alone or
a group of them together will have the intestinal fortitude—after a quarter of a century of standing in line
with their hats in their hands before the Executive in

Washington—to recapture for themselves their historic role in the Republic, remains to be seen.

The other proposal offers the greatest hope of success at the moment. It requires no constitutional amendment —only action by the people's representatives in the Congress of the United States. It is entirely within the Constitution—in fact, it is specifically provided for in our great Charter in the following words (Art. III, Sec. 2):

> In all cases affecting ambassadors, other public ministers and consuls, and those in which a state shall be party, the Supreme Court shall have original jurisdiction. In all other cases before mentioned, the Supreme Court shall have *appellate jurisdiction,* both as to law and fact, *with such exceptions, and under such regulations as the Congress shall make.*

This section means that Congress can make regulations and exceptions as to the type and kind of cases which could be taken on appeal from lower courts to the Supreme Court. In other words, Congress could say, for instance, that once a state court has upheld the constitutionality of a state sedition law, or a state school law, or once a lower federal court has upheld the right of Congress itself to protect the citizens against subversion, the matter would end right there. The Supreme Court would have no right to hear such cases on appeal and reverse the decisions. Congress could, for example, pass a law providing that the Supreme Court must not review any cases having to do with schools or education—traditionally and constitutionally always state problems. Such cases would be left where they belong—in the state courts. If an educational problem involving a federal question should come up, Congress could specify that only then would it go to a federal district court, whose judgment would be final.

The same process could be applied by Congress to laws affecting subversion—laws designed to protect us and our liberties from the onslaughts of the communist conspiracy. In fact, a committee of the American Bar Association, in July, 1957, called on Congress to pass legislation which would, in effect, wipe out the long string of procommunist decisions of the Warren Supreme Court. The Bar Association committee demanded legislation to:

Keep the FBI files confidential.

Allow schools, colleges, and bar associations to refuse employment or membership to persons who won't answer questions about past or present communist activities.

Permit congressional investigating committees to question suspected subversives as freely as they do businessmen and labor leaders.

Allow the Justice Department to question aliens awaiting deportation about any subversive associations.

Correct the Warren Court's gratuitous edict that under the Smith Act, it is all right to urge the violent overthrow of the government so long as you don't spell out how it is to be overthrown.

These recommendations of the American Bar Association committee were read by the committee's chairman, former Senator Herbert R. O'Conor, to the 3,000 delegates of the American Bar Association at its 80th annual convention in London—the same convention at which Chief Justice Warren appeared on the platform in a chocolate-colored suit to the dismay or amusement of assembled guests. The 3,000 delegates applauded Senator O'Conor's report vigorously. But its impact on the mind of the Chief Justice of the United States, so far as anybody has been able to determine, was nil.

However, the fact remains that Congress has it within its power to correct many of the evils which the packed Supreme Court has visited upon us. According to some authorities, Congress can even specify by law what constitutes "good behavior" on the part of the justices—and should they go outside or beyond those specifications, they would become answerable to the Congress in proving that they should continue to hold their high posts.

When we say that Congress has it within its power to curb the runaway Supreme Court, in the final analysis that means a power which resides in *you*—the free American citizen. Congress is always only as good or as bad as you—who elect its members and keep them in office—make it. You can sit back in complacent despair and say: "Oh, what's the use? Congress pays no attention to what we want." If you do, you have no one to blame but yourself if the Supreme Court continues to ride roughshod over your liberties. But if you and enough other Americans demand that Congress rescue from the nine usurpers on the bench the tattered charter of freedom, repair it, and restore it to the people, you will be amazed at how quickly the demand will bring action. But the demand must be persistent enough, vocal enough, and numerous enough to overcome the pressures of the loud and organized minorities who are ever vigilant in their own interests. The greater interest is the liberties of a free people— and freedom-loving people far outnumber all the vocal minorities combined. They have only to make their voices heard and their numbers felt.

There is one final proposal to reverse the usurpations of the Supreme Court. It was made by the well-known writer and commentator John T. Flynn. Aside from immediate congressional action as outlined above, it would seem to be a necessary prerequisite to all other reforms of the Court. It is that all decisions of the Supreme Court, from 1937 to the date of the adoption of the proposal, should be declared to have no force and effect as precedents in judicial or other proceedings in determining the meaning of the words, sections, and provisions of the Constitution.

The purpose here is obvious. It is to enable all future Supreme Courts, no matter how otherwise reformed, to disregard the usurpations of the Court in the last twenty years. The justices would return to the body of law and precedents set up before the usurpations began in order to decide on all future cases that would come before them.

This proposal, of course, would require a constitutional amendment. But, once again, do not despair. The amendment process seems a long one—passage by two thirds of both houses of Congress and three fourths of the states. But we have amended the Constitution twenty-two times since its adoption—in some instances with a good deal of speed—and in many cases on questions of relatively minor importance compared with the overwhelming urgency of the one which now faces us. Nowhere, at no time in our history, as we contemplate the Supreme Court and its attack on our liberties, do the words of Edmund Burke have a greater meaning for us: "All that is necessary for the triumph of evil is that good men do nothing."

## SUPREME COURT DECISIONS MENTIONED IN THIS VOLUME

| Year decided | Case | Popularly known as | Dealing with | Reference | Mentioned in text at page |
|---|---|---|---|---|---|
| 1896 | Plessy v. Ferguson | Same | Separate but equal facilities | 163 U.S. 537 | 83, 93, 107 |
| 1935 | A.L.A. Schechter Corp. v. U.S. | Sick Chicken or NRA Case | NRA and gov't. control of industry | 295 U.S. 495 | 18-20 |
| 1936 | Carter v. Carter Coal Co. | Guffey Coal Act Case | Gov't. control of coal production | 298 U.S. 238 | 20 |
| 1936 | U.S. v. Butler | AAA Case | Gov't. control of agriculture | 297 U.S. 1 | 20 |
| 1942 | A. B. Kirschbaum v. Walling | Elevator Operator Case | Interstate commerce | 316 U.S. 517 | 55 |
| 1943 | Schneiderman v. U.S. | Schneiderman Case | Citizenship of alien communists | 320 U.S. 118 | 58 |
| 1944 | Korematsu v. U.S. | Relocation Case | Rights of Japanese-American citizens | 323 U.S. 214 | 60 |
| 1945 | Bridges v. Wixon | Harry Bridges Case | Deportation | 326 U.S. 135 | 58 |
| 1952 | Youngstown Sheet & Tube v. Sawyer | Steel Case | Presidential seizure of steel mills | 343 U.S. 579 | 66, 67 |
| 1953 | Bridges v. U.S. | Harry Bridges Case | Naturalization | 346 U.S. 209 | 58 |
| 1954 | Brown v. Board of Education | Segregation Case | Schools and segregation | 347 U.S. 483 | 79-82 |
| 1954 | Phillips Petroleum v. Wisconsin | Natural Gas Case | Control of resources | 347 U.S. 672 | 133 |
| 1955 | Peters v. Hobby | Peters Case | Loyalty | 349 U.S. 331 | 119 |

| Year | Case | Short name | Subject | Citation | Pages |
|---|---|---|---|---|---|
| 1956 | Pennsylvania v. Nelson | Sedition Case | State sedition laws | 350 U.S. 497 | 119-20, 122 |
| 1956 | Cole v. Young | Cole Case | Gov't. security risks | 351 U.S. 536 | 123 |
| 1956 | Ry. Employees Dept. v. Hanson | Nebraska Labor Case | Labor unions | 351 U.S. 225 | 34, 135 |
| 1956 | Slochower v. Bd. of Higher Ed. | Slochower Case | Teachers | 350 U.S. 551 | 4, 102, 122-3, 129 |
| 1957 | Gold v. U.S. | Ben Gold Case | Noncommunist oaths | 352 U.S. 985 | 125-6 |
| 1957 | Jencks v. U.S. | Jencks Case | FBI files | 353 U.S. 657 | 108, 127 |
| 1957 | Konigsberg v. State Bar | Konigsberg Case | Practice of law | 353 U.S. 252 | 6, 126-7 |
| 1957 | Lambert v. Calif. | Calif. Felon Case | Knowledge of law | 353 U.S. 979 | 132 |
| 1957 | Mallory v. U.S. | Mallory Case | Police apprehension of criminal suspects | 352 U.S. 877 | 140-1 |
| 1957 | Penna. v. Board of Directors of City Trusts | Girard College Case | Wills and schools | 353 U.S. 230, 989 | 135-8 |
| 1957 | Sentner v. Barton | Sentner Case | Deportation of communists | 353 U.S. 963 | 127 |
| 1957 | Service v. Dulles | Service Case | Gov't. employees | 354 U.S. 363 | 124-5 |
| 1957 | Sweezy v. New Hampshire | Sweezy Case | Teachers | 354 U.S. 234 | 129 |
| 1957 | U.S. v. E. I. duPont de Nemours Co. | duPont Case | Clayton Act & "monopoly" | 353 U.S. 586 | 134-5 |
| 1957 | Watkins v. U.S. | Watkins Case | Congressional investigations | 354 U.S. 178 | 7, 27, 33, 128 |
| 1957 | Yates v. U.S. | California Communists Case | Smith Act & overthrow of gov't. | 354 U.S. 298 | 5, 130, 133, 156 |

# Index

163